Bridging Divides

BRIDGING DIVIDES
Ethno-political Leadership among the Russian Sámi

Indra Overland
and
Mikkel Berg-Nordlie

berghahn
NEW YORK • OXFORD
www.berghahnbooks.com

First published in 2012 by
Berghahn Books
www.berghahnbooks.com

© 2012, 2015 Indra Overland and Mikkel Berg-Nordlie
First paperback edition published in 2015.

Library of Congress Cataloging-in-Publication Data
Overland, Indra.
  Bridging divides : ethno-political leadership among the Russian Sámi / Indra
Overland and Mikkel Berg-Nordlie.
      p. cm.
  Includes bibliographical references and index.
  ISBN 978-0-85745-667-0 (hardback : alk. paper) -- ISBN 978-1-78238-919-
4 (paperback : alk. paper) -- ISBN 978-0-85745-668-7 (ebook)
  1. Sami (European people)--Russia (Federation)--Politics and government.
2. Sami (European people)--Russia (Federation)--Social conditions. I. Berg-
Nordlie, Mikkel. II. Title.
  DK34.S17O84 2012
  305.89'4576--dc23

                                                                    2012013685

British Library Cataloguing in Publication Data
A catalogue record for this book is available from the British Library

Printed on acid-free paper.

ISBN: 978-0-85745-667-0 hardback
ISBN: 978-1-78238-919-4 paperback
ISBN: 978-0-85745-668-7 ebook

CONTENTS

TABLES

FIGURES

ACKNOWLEDGEMENTS

This book is based on Indra Overland's PhD thesis at the Scott Polar Research Institute of the University of Cambridge. The authors rewrote and edited the original text in collaboration. Mikkel Berg-Nordlie carried out several fieldwork trips for the book during the period 2009–2011. The more recent research, and the editing process, was done as a part of the project *Russia in Pan-Sámi Politics*, which was a joint endeavour of the Norwegian Institute for Urban and Regional Research (NIBR) and the Norwegian Institute of International Affairs (NUPI). The joint project was led by Jørn Holm-Hansen, who also participated in the more recent fieldwork. Both the original PhD thesis and the joint project of NIBR and NUPI were financed by the Programme for Sámi Studies of the Research Council of Norway.

Many people have gone through the manuscript with a critical eye and provided valuable feedback, including Bård A. Berg, Susan Høivik, Jørn Holm-Hansen, Leif Rantala, Michael Rießler and Elisabeth Scheller. In addition, numerous people went over large parts of the text at earlier stages of the writing process: Oleg Andreyev, Tatiana Argounova-Low, Aileen Espiritu, Paul Fryer, Yulian Konstantinov, Igor Krupnik, Astrid Larsson-Kalvemo, Khadidjha Mattar, Maryon McDonald, Nikolay Vakhtin, Irina Vinogradova and Emma Wilson. The greatest thanks of all go to Piers Vitebsky of the University of Cambridge, who supervised the PhD upon which this book is based. Without his guidance and profound knowledge of the indigenous peoples of the Russian North, this project would never have been realized. However, none of these individuals is responsible for the contents of the book, for which the authors are solely responsible.

MAPS

Figure 0.1. Map of Sápmi

Sápmi, the traditional territory of the Sámi, extends over four countries, as shown on the map on the previous page. The black areas indicate districts in which the majority language and a Sámi language are formally of equal status. The black and dark grey areas of Norway include the Sámi Parliament electoral constituencies down to and including the South Sámi Constituency. Norway south of Sápmi constitutes an electoral constituency of its own: the South Norway Constituency. The dark grey part of Russia represents the four districts (*rayons*) currently considered official 'traditional Sámi areas' by the provincial (*oblast*) authorities. Light grey areas in Sweden, Finland and Russia are other regions often included as part of Sápmi on maps.

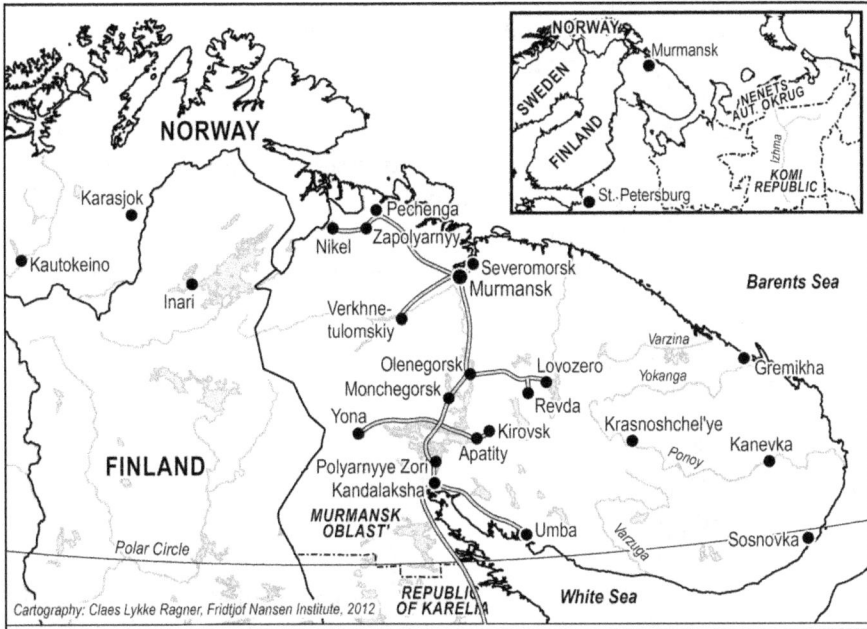

Figure 0.2. Map of the Kola Peninsula

Transcription

The first time the text mentions a place that has more than one official name – that is, both a Sámi language name and a majority-language name – it is referred to as Sámi toponym/majority-language toponym. Thereafter, we refer to the place by its Sámi name only. If the area in question does not have Sámi as a co-official language, only the majority-language toponym is used in the text. Hence, since the district which is home to Norway's Sámi University College has Sámi and Norwegian as official languages, it is referred to as 'Guovdageaidnu/Kautokeino' the first time it is mentioned, but thereafter only 'Guovdageaidnu'. However, the district known in Sámi as 'Luyavvr' or 'Lujávri' is referred to only by its Russian name 'Lovozero' as that district is not officially bilingual. Exceptions are made when quoting interviewees in order to reproduce their usage of toponyms accurately.

Table 0.1. Cyrillic–Latin Transcription

А, а	A, a
Б, б	B, b
В, в	V, v
Г, г	G, g
Д, д	D, d
Е, е	E, e or Ye, ye – the latter will be applied at the beginning of words, after vowels and after 'hard' or 'soft' signs (even in cases where these signs are not transcribed; see below).
Ё, ё	Yo, yo
Ж, ж	Zh, zh
З, з	Z, z
И, и	I, i
Й, й	Y, y
К, к	K, k
Л, л	L, l

М, м	M, m
Н, н	N, n
О, о	O, o
П, п	P, p
Р, р	R, r
С, с	S, s
Т, т	T, t
У, у	U, u
Ф, ф	F, f
Х, х	Kh, kh
Ц, ц	Ts, ts
Ч, ч	Ch, ch
Ш, ш	Sh, sh
Щ, щ	Shch, shch
Ъ, ъ	'Hard' sign, not included in transcription; except when we refer to authors' names and the titles of books. In these cases, hard signs are rendered as " (double apostrophe). The reasoning for this is included under 'Ь, ь'.
Ы, ы	Y, y
Ь, ь	'Soft' sign, not included in transcription except when we refer to authors' names and the titles of books. In these cases, soft signs are rendered as ' (single apostrophe). This has been done in order to make it easier for the reader to identify the Russian-language literature listed in the bibliography. It would make it difficult for readers to find the source literature if they have an erroneous impression of how authors' names and titles are spelled in Cyrillic. When individuals occur as both actors in the events described in the book and as authors of referenced literature, their names are written without apostrophes when mentioned in the text, but transcribed more faithfully into Cyrillic orthography in the references. Hence, if we refer to a document written by a politician whose name in Russian is written 'Ельцин', we would refer to him as 'Yel'tsin'. However, if discussing the life and actions of this politician, we would refer to him simply as 'Yeltsin' for the sake of readability.
Э, э	E, e
Ю, ю	Yu, yu
Я, я	Ya, ya

CHAPTER 1

INTRODUCTION

The Sámi are an indigenous Northern European people whose homeland, Sápmi, extends across the territories of four states: Finland, Norway, Russia and Sweden. For the Sámi of the Nordic countries, a long period of cultural repression gave way to a renaissance of sorts during the last half of the twentieth century. During the last decades of the century, their indigenous rights were recognized, they experienced a cultural and linguistic revival, and popularly elected Sámi parliaments were established in each of the three Nordic states. In contrast, the Soviet Sámi had little opportunity to develop independent ethno-political organizations and were largely isolated from their ethnic kin across the Norwegian border. The Soviet–Norwegian frontier was one of only two short stretches where the USSR and NATO shared a direct land border (the other being between Turkey and the USSR), and it remained tightly sealed until 1989.

After the Soviet Union collapsed, Russia's borders opened. In the decades that followed, the Russian Sámi attempted a linguistic revival; they began mending the Cold War scars across Sápmi and established their own independent ethno-political organizations. This period saw numerous struggles over the right to define the interests of the Russian Sámi and represent them, laying the foundations for current Russian Sámi politics.

This book tells the story of what happened once the Soviet borders opened up. In this volume, we follow the development of an ethno-political movement on the periphery of the Russian Federation: the tensions that arise when a small people attempts to organize itself, reconstitute its culture and identity and reach out across the old Iron Curtain to ethnic kin in the West. As this border has been one of the most important dividing lines in modern history, the tale of the Sámi people and their efforts to mend their divisions is a case study of not only an indigenous movement, but indeed a microcosm of Russian–Western relations, replete with idealism, opportunism, misunderstandings, cultural exchange and intended and unintended consequences.

The Russian Sámi revival has been a multifaceted one. We are particularly preoccupied with two aspects: firstly, the formation of the first post-Soviet group of Sámi leaders, whose origins are found in the Soviet Sámi intelligentsia; secondly, the consequences of the increasing contact between the Russian Sámi and their more numerous, wealthy and rights-endowed kin in the West – namely, the Nordic Sámi. These are in themselves broad fields of study, so we have narrowed our narrative down to three main themes. First, we concentrate on the initial post-Soviet attempts at linguistic revival and the close connection between this process and the emergence of a Russian Sámi ethno-political elite. We then look at the educational re-orientation of the Russian Sámi away from St. Petersburg's Herzen University and towards Sámi educational institutions in the Nordic states. Finally, we examine the founding of the first Sámi political organizations in Russia. Throughout this work, we focus on disagreements among various factions, the popular legitimacy of leaders and organizations, and problems involving the relationship between the urbanized and educated part of the Russian Sámi community and its more rural part.

Our field of study is thus Russian Sámi politics, which we define as actions linked by discourse or consequence to the situation of the Sámi people in Russia. For the purposes of this book, we also limit ourselves to the formalized Sámi ethno-political organizations on the Kola Peninsula. We try to cover both informal and formal aspects of these organizations, but we do not aim to carry out a comprehensive review of the myriad informal practices at other levels of the Russian Sámi community. As described by Yurchak (2006), such practices pervade post-Soviet society; and it would be overly ambitious to cover them all in such a volume, even for a small community like the Russian Sámi.

Our book spans the formative decades of post-Soviet Russian Sámi politics, a period that had its roots in the first signs of cultural-linguistic revitalization during the 1970s and particularly the 1980s, continued with a flurry of political activity in the 1990s, and culminated in the years around the turn of the millennium. This period is roughly analogous to the period of Russian Sámi history that Kalstad (2009: 50–55) dubbed 'the time of cultural rebirth'. According to Kalstad, this period began in approximately 1985 and ended in about 2002–03. Perestroika heralded its beginning, and its most defining event was the establishment of the Russian Sámi organization AKS in 1989, which became the hub of Russia's Sámi political life and was accepted into the cross-border Sámi Council in 1992. Kalstad considered the phase of cultural rebirth to have ended in 2002–03, asserting that a new phase had been entered – 'the return of our lands and reindeer herding' – during which time the Russian Sámi would have their last chance to return to family-based reindeer herding (and other traditional ways of life) through the *obshchina*s, which will be discussed later on in this book (Kalstad 2009: 55–72).

Kalstad passed away in 2008 (his book was published posthumously), and we therefore cannot know how he would have viewed developments in Russian Sámi politics today. For our part, we have chosen to consider the foundation of the *obshchina*s as just one (albeit important) phenomenon in a 'multipolar phase' of Russian Sámi politics which began just before the year 2000. This period is different from the preceding one in that while Russian Sámi civil society had previously been dominated by the AKS, the 1998 establishment of a second organization, OOSMO, which also aimed at organizing all the Sámi in Russia and was accepted into the Sámi Council in 2000, heralded a new era in which the landscape of Russian Sámi civil society became increasingly complex.

Following the foundation of OOSMO, several important events occurred, such as the opening of a new building for the Lovozero National Cultural Centre in 2003 (the centre had originally been established in 1994), the launching of the Kola Sámi Radio, and the establishment of the first Sámi *obshchina*s: kin- and family-based organizations aimed at ensuring the rebirth of traditional economic activities (Kalstad 2009: 54). Later in this 'multipolar' period of Russian Sámi politics, several significant institutions were created, including an official government organ at the provincial level to deal with Sámi affairs (the Murmansk Provincial Centre for Indigenous Minorities of the North), *natsional'nye kul'turnye avtonomii* (local 'national cultural autonomies' for preserving culture and language), and a Sámi youth organization (*Sam' nurash*). In later years, the Kola Sámi Assembly, an NGO-based attempt at creating a Nordic-style Sámi Parliament, was also launched; a move that was subsequently answered by the provincial authorities with the creation of the *obshchina*-based Council of Indigenous Minorities of the North (Berg-Nordlie 2011b: 62–71). At the time of writing, there are nineteen registered *obshchina*s and nine public organizations (*obshchestvennye obyedineniya*), including three national cultural autonomies (CIMN 2011a) and two structures aimed at uniting and coordinating the Russian Sámi.

Hence, from a meagre beginning in the 1980s, when no Russian Sámi political organizations existed at all, the organizational landscape passed through a phase in the 1990s in which one dominant entity existed, and ended up branching out in the 2000s into a much more diverse conglomerate of organizations and bodies, rivalling or cooperating in varying constellations.

This division of Russian Sámi political history into a pre-organizational phase, a unipolar phase (1989–1998) and a multipolar phase (1998–ongoing) is a periodization based on (and, hence, mainly relevant for) developments in civil society, official agencies and international activities.

If one were to look primarily at other sectors of Russian Sámi society, it would perhaps be more prudent to operate with different historical periodizations. For example, Konstantinov (2011: 192–198) paints a picture of the early 1990s as a time 'when all this mess began', based on rural people's experience of their socio-economic situation: with the fall of the USSR, the country underwent a systemic shock, followed by an infrastructural and economic decline that hit the rural indigenous population on the Kola Peninsula hard, creating dire problems (which have still not been solved) for the land-based traditional professions of the Sámi. If we, on the other hand, look at the Russian Sámi language situation, we see a steady decline that begins long before the fall of the USSR and continues today (see Appendix 5). This book concerns the remarkable growth of Russian Sámi political activity that took place simultaneously with these negative developments. A major task of the new group of Russian Sámi politicians has been to address these issues and, as we shall see, the birth of the movement is connected particularly intimately to worries over the fate of the group's language.

This book highlights the roots of the current civil society, which are to be found in the formative decades of the 1980s and 1990s. Disagreements and differences were also salient during this formative stage, and the events that subsequently emerged can be partially read as continuations of what happened then. Indeed, in order to understand contemporary ethno-politics among the Russian Sámi, it is vital to understand the developments during the 1990s.

Throughout this book we chart the divide between the more urban elite and the more rural groupings among the Russian Sámi, noting both the tensions and the interdependence between these two poles of the community. The 'divides' referred to in the title of this book, and to which the nascent Russian Sámi ethno-political movement had to adapt, were thus twofold: a divide between rural and urban Russian Sámi and a divide between the Russian Sámi and their ethnic kin in the Nordic countries. The most fundamental challenge facing the first post-Soviet Russian Sámi leaders was to bridge these divides.

As is common in the early stages of ethno-political movements, the Russian Sámi movement faced a representational problem during its first years due to both a clear gender imbalance and the complete dominance of educated, urban people among its leaders. The absence of activists and leaders emanating from the rural parts of the community constituted a considerable problem as these two opposite poles need each other: Without support from the majority of their constituency, an elite cannot legitimately promote an ethno-political project while, at the same time, the rank and file of an ethnic minority needs the intelligentsia, who possess resources and knowledge necessary for navigating the bureaucratic and political systems of the modern states in which they live.

Before plunging into post-Soviet ethno-politics, we present an historical account of the plight of the Russian Sámi up to the time of the Soviet collapse, then outline the basic problems the Russian Sámi faced when the socio-economic system fell apart and Russia became an independent state. Next, we examine the three previously mentioned themes, before concluding with some words on leadership legitimacy and successes in this period, the effects of cooperation with Nordic Sámi actors in the educational sphere and what all this has meant for the further development of Russian Sámi politics.

It would be no exaggeration to say that the Kola Peninsula's indigenous politics underwent a revolution through the events described in this book: a multi-level mending of the divides between East and West began, the Russian Sámi developed a civil society of their own, and people gained new confidence in their own ethnic identity. Despite teething troubles, the Russian Sámi managed to set up their own ethno-political infrastructure and, in the subsequent years, actively attempted to shape their own future as part of the border-transcending Sámi people.

About the Data Gathering and Presentation

This book has been sixteen years in the making, starting with the preparations for the first fieldwork in 1996 and ending with the publication of the book in 2012. During those sixteen years, the manuscript has gone through several intermediate stages. The book is based on Indra Overland's PhD thesis and has been rewritten by the two authors in collaboration. At the empirical level, it is based on fieldwork conducted during the 1990s (Overland) and the 2000s (Berg-Nordlie). In finalizing the text we encountered ethical and methodological issues that gave rise to much reflection and debate, which we discuss in this section.

Much of the data collection for this volume was carried out through participant observation, a method that builds upon the extended presence of the researcher in the society under study, as well as the anonymization of places and people. Overland spent more than a year on fieldwork on the Kola Peninsula, divided into four trips. His interviews were carried out as informal conversations without recourse to questionnaires or other forms of script. They were recorded when the interviewees gave permission to do so, which was usually the case.

However, some public figures and leaders of organizations were sensitive to having their interviews recorded and – in a very few cases – even reacted to having notes taken. On the other hand, as Shils (1959/1973: 125) noted, many people also gain great satisfaction from being interviewed. Numerous informants had attitudes similar to one of Barnes' (1979: 113) informants, who asked whether he thought him 'a fool whose words were not worth recording'.

At no time were interpreters used. Instead, both authors learned the language used most by the locals: Russian. Attempts were also made to learn the main Sámi language spoken on the Kola Peninsula – namely, Kildin Sámi – albeit without much success, partly because of its disuse among the Russian Sámi themselves.

Berg-Nordlie's fieldwork consisted of shorter expeditions during which individual political activists and officials (current and former) were interviewed by appointment. Informants were asked if they could be quoted with their full names, but requests for anonymity were respected. Persons interviewed in the latter round of fieldwork were given the opportunity to check their statements prior to the publication of the book.

Yet the book is not based exclusively on interviews and participant observation; it is also based on historical research using a wide array of written sources. In studies of representation, legitimacy and ethno-political leadership such as this one, the importance of drawing on all available resources and research methods has been widely acknowledged (see, for example, Medhurst and Moyser 1987: 107; Ludz quoted in Binn 1987: 223; Pridham 1987: 85–87).

In the present study, local newspapers play a particularly important role, fulfilling several critical functions. First, when discussing the activities of public figures who may be hesitant to allow conversations to be recorded, the newspapers provide extensive information about their opinions and activities. Secondly, although most of the same information is available as gossip and everyday conversation among the local population, published texts are a much more referable source of information. For example, a person interviewed anonymously may subsequently deny having said the controversial things s/he is being quoted as stating. This methodological problem is reduced significantly when the same discourses have been articulated and the same events described in publicly accessible, written documents. Allegations made in newspapers and not just in anonymous interviews also involve an ethical aspect in that they ensure that those criticized have the possibility to learn about the accusations being made and have an opportunity to counter them.

The most important newspaper as far as the Russian Sámi are concerned is *Lovozerskaya pravda*, sometimes nicknamed *Lovozerka* (e.g., N. Bogdanov 1997: 3). This newspaper, the name of which means 'the Lovozero truth', has been in print since 1935 and is by far the most comprehensive written source of information about the Russian Sámi. Large collections of back issues are readily available from, among other places, the public library in Lovozero and the Scientific Library in Murmansk.

The issue of anonymity caused much reflection and discussion during the writing and finalization of this book. It may be difficult for other researchers to double-check research when it is based on anonymous statements. Hence, the more controversial facts related in the book are generally based on newspaper references in addition to our own interviews. As a part of this approach, we have sought to avoid quoting denunciations by anonymous informants of named private individuals.

Anonymous interviews are a better source when it comes to mapping discursive landscapes – namely, how people think and talk about certain issues or phenomena or certain categories of people. Attitudes towards 'the leaders' as a group of people are important in this book as popular mobilization and the maintenance of popular legitimacy are vital factors in a nascent ethno-political movement. The utilization of intensive fieldwork in diverse Sámi communities has proved to be a good source for gathering such information. Interviews were conducted in the urban centres of Murmansk Province, the main Russian Sámi town of Lovozero, as well as in smaller villages and roadless settlements on the Kola Peninsula. They have brought to this book an incomparable source of information about attitudes articulated among the Russian Sámi.

Where interviews have been anonymized, this has been done thoroughly. In most cases, only minor personal data about the interviewees are provided. In a few cases, the gender, occupation, age, place of residence or similar indicators of identity have been altered in the hope of avoiding the type of criticism levelled most famously against Vidich and Bensman, whose Springdale Study (1958) is probably the best-known case involving issues of anonymity in an academic study of a small community. The subjects were given pseudonyms, but the town in which the study was carried out was nonetheless readily identifiable, as were many of those who participated in it. Some of those who had been studied, later reacted by ridiculing the academics and their research in a Fourth of July parade (Kelman 1982: 84–85; Burgess 1995: 188; Barnes 1979: 136). In making changes to avoid the problems of the Springdale Study, we have taken care not to affect the overall picture in terms of the gender profile or other factors among informants.

Finally, a question emerges of possible damage done to individual political activists through the description of actions committed by them that may be perceived as inappropriate or by pointing out widespread negative discourses about them. The observation of people's behaviour in the public sphere does not require their consent (Capron 1982: 215; Barnes 1979: 166). Such a viewpoint does not rest upon an argument about the implicit consent of those being studied and the benign intentions of those studying. It is merely based on the view that the public sphere should remain open to public opinion and inspection (Medhurst and Moyser 1987: 106; Rainwater and Pittman 1967: 365; Galliher 1973).

Note that – in line with Shils' (1959/1973: 130) definition – here 'public sphere' does not mean merely the sphere in which one is open to the scrutiny of society in general, as when walking down the street. Rather, the term here refers to opinions published or expressed from a position of power and/or responsibility as well as acts carried out in connection with such a position: 'When actors become involved in government and business or other organizations where they are accountable to the public, no right of privacy applies to conduct in such roles' (Barnes 1979: 166). Those individuals whom we treat as public figures have themselves chosen to enter the public sphere, whether by taking up official leadership posts, making public speeches, expressing strong political views in articles and interviews, representing the Russian Sámi at conferences and in pan-Sámi political organs, or applying for support in the name of the Russian Sámi and their culture.

The impossibility of hiding the identities of public figures in such small, unique places is reflected in, for example, Golovnev's (1997: 157, 160) perceptive four-pronged study of Nenets, Selkup, Khanty and Mansi communities. Golovnev does not mention leaders by name, but describes them to a degree that allows recognition; he further makes unveiled references to the names of their clans and villages. Hence, they are identifiable in the surroundings where this matters most: at the local level. Ingold's work *The Skolt Lapps Today* (1976) was criticized on this point: 'There are many shrewd judgements, a few hasty conclusions and obvious prejudice against, for instance, the successful "big-men" and "speculators" among reindeer owners, against "bourgeois" values and immigrant professionals as "elite". The eloquent local leader, unnamed but holding named posts, is denounced repeatedly, as if by a participant in the scene' (Lindgren 1977: 494). Note that this criticism occurs on two levels: firstly, the recognizability of those against whom accusations are being made; secondly, the perception that the author himself is denouncing certain groups and activists.

In this book we identify some protagonists in the formative decades of Russian Sámi politics by their full names because attempts at anonymization would be pointless. Not only would these figures be easily identifiable anyway, but they have also put themselves in positions where democracy demands that they must be subjected to public scrutiny. On the other hand, we have no desire to denounce – or glorify – any political actors. Therefore, we have tried to be fair when relating criticism against some of them by putting their actions into context and shedding light on the opinions of all sides in these formative conflicts of Russian Sámi politics.

Reflexivity about the methods of research as well as forms of representation is not only a methodological and ethical matter, but also a theoretical one that cannot be reduced to questions of anonymity. Therefore, we also find it appropriate to note here that we have tried and – as far as we can judge ourselves – managed to strike a balance between thoroughly involving ourselves in the everyday lives of the Russian Sámi and avoiding developing personal allegiances to particular groups among the Russian Sámi. We have spoken to a large number of Russian Sámi, participated in their everyday lives over long periods of time, and taken part in political meetings, trips and conferences, but always as relatively passive and hopefully neutral outsiders. The fact that one of us is an ethnic Sámi and the other is not should hopefully also help balance and nuance the text.

As Russian Sámi politics, like most indigenous politics, is centred on the idea of cultural survival and revival, the word 'culture' is central to our description and analysis. Therefore, before delving into our analysis, we explicitly define 'Sámi culture' as the practices and symbols considered to be 'Sámi' by the people who consider themselves Sámi. Yet at a functional level, culture is also something more in this context: a key reference point in an ethno-political discourse. 'Sámi culture' is that which has to be protected, developed, treasured and supported. Without a 'Sámi culture' – symbols and practices that the Sámi may recognize as their own – it is assumed that the Sámi will eventually die out as an identity collective. The protection and furthering of 'Sámi culture' holds a central place in the political project this book concerns.

CHAPTER 2

WHO ARE THE RUSSIAN SÁMI?

The Sámi, Their Territory and Their Language

The Sámi are the indigenous people of Scandinavia, Finland and Russia's Kola Peninsula. In older literature, they are referred to as 'Lapps', a word first recorded in Russian chronicles as 'Lop' and that may have originated in medieval times in northeastern areas of Europe, such as Staraya Ladoga (Hansen and Olsen 2004: 45–51). Since 'Lapp' is considered a derogatory term by many members of the group, it has now largely been replaced by 'Sámi', the people's own name for themselves in the North Sámi language.

The Sámi people's traditional area of habitation is called 'Sápmi' (once again, in the North Sámi language). No official outer boundaries for Sápmi have been determined in Norway and Sweden, but it is common to include areas as far south as Lake Femunden in Norway and Härjedalen in Sweden. The Finnish authorities have defined the northernmost fringes of their Lapland Province as the Sámi Domicile Area, while the Russian authorities have recognized the districts of Lovozero, Kola, Kovdor and Ter as 'traditional Sámi areas' (Kalstad 2006: 19).[1] Finnish and Russian delimitations of Sámi areas are more conservative than many unofficial maps of Sápmi, which at times include the entire Finnish province of Lapland and most, or all, of Murmansk Province. In addition to the part of the Sámi population living in Sápmi, a significant proportion of the Nordic Sámi has migrated further south, with particularly large groups coalescing in the capitals of their respective countries (i.e., Helsinki, Oslo and Stockholm).

Population estimates for the Sámi are entirely dependent on the criteria applied and thus vary greatly. On its homepages, the Nordic Sámi Institute (2008) presents estimates varying between 64,000 (data from the Finnish Sámi Parliament) and 100,000 (Norwegian Sámi Parliament).

Registered and eligible voters for Sámi Parliamentary elections number 13,890 in Norway (Norwegian Sámi Parliament 2011), 7,812 in Sweden (Swedish Sámi Parliament 2009) and 5,317 in Finland (Finnish Sámi Parliament 2007).[2] However, these last figures are a poor indicator of the number of Sámi in the world today as they reflect little more than the number of Sámi individuals who actively support the institutions of self-determination and have undertaken the necessary practical steps to register to vote in Sámi elections. For further population estimates, see Appendix 2.

The Sámi languages belong to the western Finno-Ugric branch of the Uralic language family. The closest languages are those of the Baltic-Finnic family. They are also related to, among others, Mordvin, Mari, Komi and Udmurt; like most Uralic languages, these are minority languages in the Russian Federation (Nickel 1994: 8–9). The variations among the different Sámi languages (often erroneously referred to as 'dialects') are in fact so great that speakers using certain Sámi languages are unable to understand one another (Beach 1994: 157). The Sámi languages may be grouped into two or three main categories: South Sámi in the broader sense (including South Sámi in the narrow sense and Ume Sámi), Central Sámi (including Lule Sámi, North Sámi and Pite Sámi) and East Sámi (including Akkala Sámi, Inari Sámi, Kildin Sámi, Skolt Sámi and Ter Sámi) (Nickel 1994: 7). It is also common to consider Central and South Sámi as forming the broader category of 'Western Sámi', separate from the Eastern Sámi languages. Dialectal variations also occur within the languages, particularly in North Sámi (Magga 2002: 11–12, 14–15).

Estimates of the number of Sámi speakers vary as widely as the estimates as to how many people consider themselves Sámi (Nordic Sámi Institute 2005). According to some, as many as 35,000 people can speak a Sámi language (Magga, in Svonni 1996: 110). However, the 1999–2000 Sámi Language Council of Norway's assessment of the Sámi language situation in selected regions of Norway[3] identified 25,000 people (17 per cent of the population of that area) who were able to understand a conversation in Sámi. It is important to note that this assessment left out several areas of Norwegian Sápmi as well as the Norwegian capital Oslo and surrounding municipalities, where many Sámi speakers live (Report to Parliament No. 55 2000–2001). According to the Nordic Sámi Institute, the Swedish Sámi Parliament operates with an estimated 30,000 to 40,000 Sámi speakers in the world while the Finnish Sámi Parliament operates with between 30,000 and 50,000.

North Sámi is the native Sámi language of northernmost Norway, Sweden and Finland and is by far the most actively and widely used of the Sámi languages. It has several dialects, all of which are mutually intelligible. In contrast, only approximately 2,000 South Sámi live in Norway and Sweden put together, of whom about 500 actually speak South Sámi (Nordic Sámi Institute 2005). Between the northern and southern cultural linguistic areas of Sápmi, three 'belts' exist and are inhabited by other Sámi sub-groups: the Ume Sámi, the Pite Sámi, and the Lule Sámi. The Lule Sámi language is the major group of these three; according to the Swedish Sámi Parliament, it is spoken by about 2,000 individuals (Nordic Sámi Institute 2005). Thus, North Sámi dominates among the Sámi languages.

The Sámi of Russia have traditionally spoken various dialects of East Sámi. The Swedish Sámi Parliament estimates that fewer than 1,600 individuals in the world speak East Sámi dialects today. The languages found on the Russian side of the border are Kildin, Ter, Skolt and Akkala. In Russian, these are called *kildinskiy, yokangskiy, notozerskiy* and *babinskiy*, which respectively refer to Kildin, an island off the Murman Coast (the northern seacoast border of the Kola Peninsula); Yokanga, the name of a river on the northeastern Kola Peninsula and the former name of the village of Ostrovnoy, where the Gremikha military base is located; Notozero, a lake in north-western Murmansk Province; and Babino in the southwestern Kovdor District.

Recent research by Scheller (2011: 86–91) indicates that approximately 700 people have some knowledge of Kildin, 100 of whom are active speakers. Skolt Sámi has no active speakers in Russia, but about twenty people know some of the language. However, communities in the West speak and/or understand it, meaning the total number of people knowledgeable in Skolt Sámi ranges between 300 and 500 (Scheller 2004: 9–11). As for Ter Sámi, only one or two active speakers exist and perhaps forty in total have some knowledge of the language. Akkala Sámi has no active speakers, and only two known individuals are familiar with the language to a certain extent (Scheller 2011: 90–92). A group of Sámi who spoke a coastal dialect of North Sámi, the so-called Filmans, also used to live on the Kola Peninsula; however, this cultural-linguistic Russian Sámi sub-group is now lost (Scheller 2004: 11; Leinonen 2008). In recent decades, a compound of Kildin sub-dialects has been used as the main basis of new dictionaries and teaching materials in an effort to revive the language in Russia.

Nordic Sámi Politics since the 1950s

Whatever the actual size of the total Sámi population, it is clear that the Norwegian group is the largest and the Russian one by far the smallest. The vast majority of the Sámi have lived in Nordic social democracies since the Second World War. After the war, the Nordic Sámi experienced a gradual turnaround in governmental policy, from assimilative pressure to greater – although far from unlimited – support for their rights as an ethnic minority and an indigenous people. Much of this development can be credited to the numerous independent Sámi organizations that developed during the same period (for some overviews see Beach 1994: 186; Swedish Institute 1991: 2; Hætta 1994: 158; Otnes 1970: 174–177; Stordahl 1994: 59; Lasko and Osherenko 1999: 21).

International Sámi conferences and institutions have appeared parallel to the national Sámi organizations. The Nordic Sámi Council (*Nordisk sameråd – Sámeráđđi*) was founded at the second Nordic Sámi Conference in Kárášjohka/Karasjok, Norway, in 1956 (Eidheim 1985: 156). The first programme of principles for Sámi politics was agreed upon at the Nordic Sámi Conference in Váhčir/Gällevare, Sweden, in 1971 and included the statement that 'we are a people with its own area of habitation, its own language, and its own cultural and social structure' (Hætta 1994: 158) – an expression of the greatly heightened self-confidence of the Sámi movement. Although this was initially controversial among the Sámi (Berg-Nordlie and Schou 2011: 12–13), it has gradually become a generally accepted ideological principle among politically active Sámi that they represent not just an ethnic minority, but also an indigenous people in their own right and that their group is therefore entitled not just to cultural survival, but also to some degree of self-determination within the political frameworks of existing states. Another underlying ideological current in modern Sámi politics is what we may call 'pan-Sámism', which refers to a general desire for increased international Sámi cooperation and the harmonization of laws and policies relating to the Sámi in the four states in which they reside (cf. Berg-Nordlie 2011b: 56; 2012: 437–438).

A major turning point in the relations of the Nordic Sámi with their nation states occurred during and in the aftermath of the Alta Dam Affair in North Norway. Due to its great importance for the development of the complex Nordic Sámi political structure, which in turn has become one of the main influences on Russian Sámi politics since 1989, we devote some space here to the issues surrounding the dam. The 1979–1982 political turmoil over the Alta Dam was the most serious open conflict between the Nordic Sámi and any of their respective nation states during the past century (Brantenberg 1985: 23). Sámi resistance to the dam included activists sending a delegation to the Pope (Brantenberg 1985: 28), conducting hunger strikes outside the Norwegian parliament in Oslo, and extensive recourse to forms of civil disobedience such as chaining themselves to machinery at the building site. The main demands were that construction of the dam be stopped and that Sámi land rights and cultural rights be recognized, a democratically elected organ be established to represent the Sámi and the Sámi be officially be recognized as a 'people' (Magga

1994: 46). At the height of the conflict, more than a quarter of the total police force of Norway was relocated to the small town of Alta in order to put down the protests and demands (Burger 1987: 180). Particularly informative sources on the affair include Paine's (1982) book on the issue, *Dam a River, Damn a People?* Bjørklund and Brantenberg's (1981) persuasive defence of the reindeer herders' case in terms of the flexibility needed for complex pastoral migratory systems and Minde's (2003) article on the Alta Dam affair, 'indigeneism' and its effect on Sámi politics.

The alliance of Sámi activists, leftists and environmentalists lost the struggle over the dam as such, which was opened in 1987, but a much smaller area than originally planned was flooded and the Sámi village of Máze/Masi was spared (Hætta 1994: 130). The conflict also brought unparalleled attention to Sámi grievances, propelling the movement for self-determination and cultural revitalization to a higher level. A commission was established to consider the rights of the Sámi people, and Sámi parliaments were inaugurated across the Nordic countries.

The first Nordic democratically elected and representative Sámi organ had already been set up in 1973 in Finland. The Norwegian and Swedish Sámi Parliaments were opened in 1989 and 1993, respectively, and the Finnish 'Sámi Delegation' reorganized into the Sámi Parliament of Finland in 1995 (Josefsen 2007: 18–21). With this, the great majority of the Sámi people had achieved similar political institutions despite being divided by state borders. The three Sámi parliaments are official advisory and participatory organs, with a certain amount of funding at their disposal for the benefit of the Sámi people. The Norwegian Sámi Parliament is arguably the most influential of the three, among other things because the Finnmark Act of 2005 gave it a certain amount of influence over natural resources in Finmárku/Finnmark County. These parliaments reflect the exceptional success of the Nordic Sámi relative to most other indigenous groups in the world in terms of negotiating a new position for themselves. It must be noted, though, that despite the development of political structures for indigenous representation, many important issues facing the Nordic Sámi remain unsolved, for example the issue of indigenous fishing rights in Norway.

Over the past twenty years, structures have gradually evolved for border-transcending cooperation among the Sámi parliaments. Representatives from these three institutions attend regular meetings (the Sámi Parliamentary Council, established in 2000), and all Sámi parliament representatives in the Nordic countries attend trilateral plenary meetings (the Sámi Parliamentary Conference, first organized in 2005). Since 2000, annual meetings have been held between the Sámi Parliament presidents and the Nordic ministers responsible for Sámi affairs (Berg-Nordlie 2012: 442–445, 447–448; Sámi Parliamentary Conference 2005; Sámi Parliamentary Council 2006; Nordic Cooperation on Sámi Issues 2000).

In addition to these new official institutions and the extant Sámi civil society, the last third of the 1900s saw a steady growth of Sámi-oriented educational institutions in the Nordic countries. The University of Tromsø, located in the largest city of North Norway, was founded in 1968 and rapidly became a hub for Sámi research and education. A Nordic Sámi Institute was founded in the town of Guovdageaidnu/Kautokeino in 1973, and a Sámi University College was established there sixteen years later. Additional academic institutions on the Nordic side of Sápmi that have a special focus on Sámi affairs include the Árran Lule Sámi Centre (Ájluokta/Drag, Norway), Gáldu Resource Centre for the Rights of Indigenous Peoples (Guovdageaidnu, Norway), the International Centre for Reindeer Husbandry (Guovdageaidnu), Sámi Educational Centres of Johkamohkki/Jokkmokk (Sweden), Anár/Inari (Finland) and the University of Lapland (Rovaniemi, Finland).

The Russian Sámi and Their Nordic Kin

Until the late 1980s, the Russian Sámi were isolated from the events discussed above. While Sámi individuals of Norway, Sweden and Finland could move unfettered back and forth across the borders (the status of Nordic Sámi rights to practice traditional, border-transcending economic activities is a different story), the Russian Sámi were confined to the Soviet Union, where they were categorized as one of the twenty-six official 'Small Peoples' of the North. Although this status entailed them to certain beneficial governmental policies, they had no opportunities to develop independent organizations or network with their kin abroad. While the Nordic Sámi spearheaded a renaissance of their own in the West, developing their own organizational infrastructure and border-transcending networks, the Russian Sámi were not allowed to take part in this. The central modern symbols of Sámi nationhood were likewise also primarily created in the Nordic part of Sápmi and only later imported into the Russian side; the Sámi flag and the lyrics of the Sámi anthem were agreed upon without the Russian Sámi's participation in 1986, although the decisions concerning the song's melody and the creation of a border-transcending Sámi People's Day were made at a conference in 1992 at which the Russian Sámi were represented (Nordisk sameråd 1987; Rantala 2004).

In short, the Russian Sámi have experienced their own particular version of a recurrent problem in Russian history: the conviction that there is a need to 'catch up' with the West after lengthy periods of isolation. The Nordic side has become a 'centre' in Sápmi relative to the Russian 'periphery': most institutions are located on the Nordic side, important symbols are of Nordic Sámi origin, and the political strategies of the Russian Sámi are often informed by Nordic Sámi successes (such as the desire to create a Sámi Parliament in Russia, cf. Berg-Nordlie 2011b: 54–58).

This tendency to look westwards is perhaps even more pronounced than it would otherwise have been due to the small size of the Russian Sámi people. Indeed, the clear majority of the border-transcending Sámi people live in the Nordic countries (see Appendix 2 for estimates of the Sámi population). For the fewer than 2,000 individuals in Russia who hold Sáminess as their primary ethnic identity, building a functioning ethnic civil society and effectively engaging in politics are challenging tasks. Through contacts with the Nordic Sámi, the Russian side of Sápmi is in many ways bringing in resources from abroad – symbolically in the sense of a self-image as belonging to a much larger people and through the moral support given by their Nordic kin, as well as more practically through other kinds of assistance that may come in handy for a people which is small even as North Russian indigenous minorities go.

When the days of the Iron Curtain came to an end, the Russian Sámi finally got their chance to seek a closer relationship with the foreign majority of their ethnic group. As Vitebsky (1992: 224) wrote of this period, 'ethnic groups and indeed all Soviet citizens, have thus been presented with a situation which arises in history only rarely: they are poised at a decisive moment in the development of the encapsulating state which gives them the possibility of renegotiating their own position in the overall picture'.

The AKS (*Assotsiatsiya kolskikh saamov*, Association of the Kola Sámi) was founded in 1989 and became the main representative organ of the Russian Sámi. The AKS achieved observer status in the Nordic Sámi Council when the Soviet Union opened up. Vasiliy Selivanov served as the first Soviet Sámi delegate to the Nordic Sámi Conference in 1983, and Eduard Yulin represented them in 1989. In 1992, the Nordic Sámi Conference approved of the AKS as members of the Nordic Sámi Council, which led to 'Nordic' being dropped from the name (Rantala 2004: Beach 1994: 149). By 1994, significant contact was occurring across this formerly impenetrable border (Rantala 1994a: 317). In 1998, a new Sámi organization appeared on the Kola Peninsula, calling itself OOSMO (*Obshchestvennaya organizatsiya saamov murmanskoy oblasti*, Public Organization of the Sámi of Murmansk Province), competing with the AKS. In 2000, the Sámi Council approved the OOSMO application for membership (Rantala 2004: 12).

The initial contacts between the modern organizations of Nordic and Russian Sámi were made at a time when Russia was plunging into a period of economic ruin, which resulted in the Nordic Sámi playing an important role in providing funding for projects, humanitarian aid and opportunities for travelling to the West, in addition to readymade political symbols and an infusion of ethnic self-awareness. In this book, we focus on what happened in these formative years, but as Humphrey (1995: 1) pointed out, on the general subject of Russian political identity, 'it is absolutely impossible to understand the present situation unless you know about the socialist past'. This is true of Russian Sámi affairs as well. Accordingly, this chapter offers a brief account of Kola Sámi history.

However, we are not ready to start that account yet, for thus far we have introduced the Russian Sámi solely as a sub-set of the Sámi. In order to understand the ethno-political development of the group since 1989, it is necessary to realize that there are at least two main political and identity alternatives available to them, apart from Russianization: the pan-Sámi movement and the post-Soviet Northern Peoples movement. These identity alternatives are not necessarily in conflict, but they are not identical; both are important and need to be presented. Thus, in the following section, we provide our second introduction to the Kola Sámi, this time as a Russian indigenous group inhabiting the Kola Peninsula.

The Kola Peninsula: Indigenous and Non-indigenous Minorities

The Kola Peninsula

The traditional territory of the Russian Sámi is the Kola Peninsula. Most of this area lies north of the Arctic Circle, but the climate is softened by the warm current of the Gulf Stream, especially along the northern coast of the peninsula, and few areas of permafrost exist (Kiselev 1988: 9). The area includes more than 130,000 rivers and lakes if the smallest ones are included (Doiban, Pretes and Sekarev 1992: 14). Parts of the peninsula still have large numbers of game, including bear, wolf and elk, in addition to an abundance of mineral resources that has given rise to a large mining and processing industry. In fact, 'seventy-five per cent of all the minerals in the periodic system are found in mineable concentrations on the [Kola] Peninsula' (Hansen 1998: 14).

As the Kola Peninsula is the most industrialized area in the entire Arctic (Doiban, Pretes and Sekarev 1992: 7; Nuttall 1998: 13), some areas have been totally devastated by pollution, especially around factory towns like Nikel and Monchegorsk. Most of the industrial development and environmental degradation is concentrated in a belt of urbanization along the north–south axis from the city of Murmansk to St. Petersburg (Konstantinov 1999: 3) whereas the eastern part of the peninsula has remained largely undeveloped. The most important exception to this rule is the sizeable nuclear submarine base at what is usually referred to as Gremikha (also known as Ostrovnoy, Yokangskaya baza and Murmansk-140) on the eastern part of the northern coast (Rantala, in Konstantinov 1999: 25). In addition, numerous military installations are located in other parts, giving the peninsula what some have deemed to be the highest concentration of nuclear weapons in the world (see Doiban, Pretes and Sekarev 1992: 9; Konstantinov 1999: 25).

One of the most dramatic instances of the Soviet environmental destruction on the Kola Peninsula was the testing of two nuclear explosives for non-military purposes in the Khibiny mountain range near the industrial cities of Kirovsk and Apatity in the 1970s (Sarv 1996: 138). In addition, a nuclear threat is posed by the Russian Northern Fleet, the Polyarnyye Zori nuclear plant, and two major storage sites for ballistic missile warheads near Revda (Nilsen and Bøhmer 1994: 73; see also Appendix 3).

Murmansk Province is almost isomorphic with the Kola Peninsula. In 1927, when the province was known as Murmansk *guberniya*, it had 23,000 inhabitants, some 8,000 to 9,000 of whom were living in the city of Murmansk (Kiselev 1997: 3). Between 1927 and 1938, the population of Murmansk *okrug* (area) grew tenfold, and numerous new towns were built on the peninsula, including Kirovsk, Monchegorsk, Polyarnyy, Afrikanda and Kildinstroy (Kiselev 1997: 3). Like much of the former Soviet North, Murmansk Province experienced a sharp reversal of earlier immigration during the 1990s. Estimates vary, but according to Sokolova and Yakovlev (1998: 6) the official population of the *oblast* in 1995 was 1,091,500, down 6 per cent since 1989. The 2002 all-Russian census indicated that 892,534 people were living in the province. A large military population is sometimes included in estimates for the province, but its size is even more difficult to estimate than that of the civilian population. The city of Murmansk is the capital of the province and a strategically and economically significant port for Russia. With 336,137 inhabitants, it is home to slightly less than half of the population of the province, according to the 2002 census.

The 2002 census also indicated that a total of 1,769 people in Murmansk Province referred to themselves as Sámi. In addition, some Sámi live in other sub-units of the Russian Federation, although only three locations have a Sámi population above 10: St. Petersburg (71), Leningrad Province (15) and Moscow (12). A total of 1,991 people identified themselves as Sámi in Russia in 2002.[4] This number needs to be understood in light of the fact that it was not possible to choose multiple ethnic identities; one could, for example, not register as both ethnic Russian (*russkiy*) and Sámi, which means that the number of Sámi in the census only reflects those whose indigenous identity is strong enough to warrant not choosing '*russkiy*' or for that matter 'Komi' or any other ethnic identity. Most of the Kola Sámi live in the district of Lovozero and are concentrated in the eponymous administrative centre, which in 2002 had a population of 3,943. The district had a total population of 14,311, of which the majority (10,368) lived in the largest settlement Revda (see Appendix 2 for further population data).

The village of Lovozero, situated about 200 km southeast of the city of Murmansk, is sometimes referred to as the 'capital' of Russian Sápmi (Arvola 1990: 4; Cherkasskiy 1998: 3). The Lovozero district constitutes 37 per cent of Murmansk Province (Sokolova and Yakovlev 1998: 13; Kuznetsova 1989: 1) and is the largest district on the peninsula, encompassing its central and eastern parts. It includes a large part of the peninsula's non-industrialized areas, which are still useful for reindeer herding and fishing, as well as many of the mineral resources attractive for industrialization. The two remaining collective farms seriously engaged in large-scale reindeer herding are in the Lovozero District: one is based in the village of Lovozero itself, the other further east in Krasnoshchelye, the largest of three roadless villages in the district. With the advent of the *obshchina*s in the new millennium, several groups of Sámi sought to return to family-based reindeer herding. The first *obshchina* was established in 2002 with help from, among others, the Norwegian Sámi academic Johan Albert Kalstad. As of 2011, however, no *obshchina*s on the Kola have succeeded in establishing large-scale reindeer husbandry. One of the main problems is gaining access to land as well as dealing with other bureaucratic difficulties (Kalstad 2009: 58–71).

Outside the district of Lovozero, the most important locations of Sámi settlement on the Kola Peninsula are the districts of Kola and Kovdor, as well as Murmansk city. Other notable cities in the province, all of them with some Sámi inhabitants, include Apatity, Severomorsk, Monchegorsk and Olenegorsk. The majority of the population on the Kola Peninsula consists of people who identify themselves as *russkiye* (Russians in the narrow, ethnic sense), Ukrainians and others who have arrived since the Second World War. Both locals on the Kola Peninsula and many authors writing on other parts of the post-Soviet North use the general term 'Russian' to refer to any such immigrants belonging to the larger Slavic ethnic groups or nations from the European part of the former USSR. Since this usage, albeit inaccurate, is also common among the Russian Sámi (especially in distinguishing broadly between indigenous and non-indigenous people), we retain it here; however, as the term is not entirely accurate, we will continue to use it with quotation marks.

Pomors, Izhma Komi and Nenets also live on the Kola Peninsula. The Pomors consider themselves to be the descendants of the first Russian migrants to the northern coast. According to Konstantinov (1999: 8), their numbers on the Kola Peninsula are roughly equivalent to those of the Sámi. The approximately 1,800 Komi are the descendants of migrants from the area around the Izhma River in the Komi Republic (see Fig. 0.2), most of whom came to the Kola Peninsula between the 1880s and the Russian Revolution. The small number of Nenets (roughly 200, according to Konstantinov 1999: 8) came with them as serfs or menial labourers for their large-scale reindeer-herding operations.

An approximately equal number of people on the Kola Peninsula identify themselves as Komi and Sámi, with some sources suggesting that the Komi even slightly outnumber the Sámi (Sokolova and Yakovlev 1998: 6). The Komi are more concentrated in the Lovozero District, while the Sámi are spread throughout most of the towns and settlements on the peninsula. By the end of the 1990s, the Komi numerically equalled the Sámi in Lovozero, and in roadless Krasnoshchelye they constituted the largest group. Because the Komi are involved in reindeer herding and fishing like the Sámi, living in the same places and using the same resources, they are of particular relevance to our account. The heavy intermingling of the groups should also be borne in mind, as many people belonging to one of the groups also have connections to the other. Therefore, the presence of the Komi adds to the complexity of the Sámi identity.

Inter-ethnic Relations and Hierarchies in the Towns and Villages

Though far less impressive in numbers than the 'Russians', the entry of the Komi on the scene had a major impact on the Sámi (Hallström 1911: 241, 275). Unlike the Pomor and more recent Russian migrants, the Komi were heavily involved in reindeer herding (Kotov 1987: 11). Moreover, they practised a more capital-intensive form of reindeer husbandry, concentrating on organization and control, with Nenets labour brought along to carry out much of the actual herding (Konakov, Kotov and Rochev 1984: 15; Hallström 1911: 242). They moved into the heart of the Sámi settlement in the centre and east of the Kola Peninsula, particularly along the Ponoy River (Zherebtsov 1982: 197), competing directly with the Sámi for pasture, fish and game.

Over time, many Sámi ended up placing their herds under Komi administration and providing the Komi with herding labour (Zherebtsov 1982: 201). Yet it should also be noted that some Komi worked for Sámi herd owners as well, although they usually established their own independent herds rapidly (Hallström 1911: 294). According to Kiselev (1994c: 4) and many Sámi, some Komi did so by stealing from the herds owned by the Sámi and to some extent the Pomors, although the latter owned fewer reindeer. The result was growing animosity between the Sámi and the Komi, with the former applying to the authorities to stop the Komi from settling on their peninsula and the Komi lobbying for the right to do so (Zherebetsov 1982: 196; Kiselev 1994a: 4). Some Sámi still maintain that the arrival of the Komi was a fatal blow to them.

For many years Lovozero remained a divided village, with the Sámi living on the right bank of the Virma River and the Komi on the left bank (Zherebtsov 1982: 200; Konakov, Kotov and Rochev 1984: 9). The prejudice connected to that division can still be found among a few locals. As one Lovozero Sámi explained:

> The Komi were forbidden people here. The Sámi chased them away. ... And therefore they didn't live here, but somewhere at a distance behind the village. They lived thirty kilometres away from the village ... in those tents. It was only later that they started building the houses ... on the other side of the river. ... I remember, on the other side there was just one big swamp. ... It's only now that streets and so on have been built. I remember it in the 1960s, when I came here to go to the internat [boarding school]. I saw all those marshy back streets of theirs. You'd go over, and there was, how shall I put it? – just muck.

Conversely, a Lovozero Komi recounted what she had read about Lovozero in an old book (Ivanov-Dyatlov 1928). According to that account, on the Sámi side of the stream,

> ... stood their dwellings. In the dwellings were fires with open outlets, and around the houses there were no garden plots at all. ... And in front of the homes there was like a small corridor, and in that corridor they kept dogs and sheep, and there were no other buildings, just dirt. ... And then what did the [Komi] Izhemtsy side look like? First of all, the houses were large, with lots of windows and very many side buildings and large garden plots. They were already growing potatoes. Of course every house had a banya [similar to a sauna], naturally a toilet, and places to keep the cattle and sheep.

The still-existing residue of such hostile mirror images – albeit notably only among a small minority – stems from the subtle continuation of the conflict during the Soviet period. Still closely entangled in the reindeer-herding sphere, the rivalry between the Sámi and Komi to some extent continued, transposed from family control over pastures to positions in the *sovkhozes*. Komi individuals were often accepted by the system more readily than the Sámi, who suffered from being at the bottom of an ethnic status hierarchy, together with the small number of Kola Nenets. In this system, 'Russians' were at the top, Komi in the middle, and Sámi at the bottom (Rantala, in Konstantinov 1999: review pages; Kolpakova 1991: 2; see also Nystad 1999: 4–5; Konstantinov 1997: 14. Also see Appendix 4 for some examples).

Hence, along with 'Russians', many Komi could be found in the middle to higher echelons of the *sovkhozes* and municipal authorities (Rantala, in Konstantinov 1999: review pages; Kolpakova 1991: 2), which inevitably led to further resentment. As one of our Sámi informants put it:

> – Look at what happened, now they are the masters. ... Their parents gave them the opportunity to go to university ... the Komi, the Russians. But our parents didn't give us anything, because they died [during the repression].

– But many people died, also Russians and Komi.

– Not as many of them died. They worked the black market, they ran away, away from the war. … So we missed the opportunity, and now we stand where we stand, trying to revive, to stand on our own feet.

The pattern of Komi being favoured for leadership positions goes all the way back to the first Soviet institutions on the Kola Peninsula. For example, according to Kiselev, the first official Native Council in Lovozero was headed by a Komi; when the Lovozero District was established in 1927, the first mayor was a Komi (Kiselev 1994c: 4; Kiselev 1994d: 3). Several leader figures with both Komi and Sámi roots have emerged and continue to emerge among the Sámi – including in the Sámi ethnic revival (Rantala, in Konstantinov 1999: review pages), although this probably just reflects the high degree of intermarriage between the groups, which has resulted in a situation in which many of the Kola Peninsula's inhabitants today are of both Komi and Sámi backgrounds. This situation is comparable to the mixing of people of Sámi and Kven background in Norway, with the Kvens also being a more recently immigrated Finno-Ugric ethnic group.

Similar stratification existed in many other parts of the Soviet Union. For example, writing about the Selkup village of Taz, Golovnev (1997: 160) notes that recent newcomers – Russians, Byelorussians, Ukrainians – constitute the overwhelming majority of the population. 'Here interethnic relations underscore the marginal position of the indigenous people. In this village the Selkup tend to hold low-status jobs requiring unskilled or manual labour. The Newcomers often treat the natives with disdain or even scorn and are uninterested in their lives'. Likewise, Humphrey (1991: 12) notes resentment among young Tuvinians towards Russians because of their advantages and dominance in former state enterprises. Schindler (1997: 200; 1993: 598) states that Chukotka *sovkhoz* directors are exclusively Russian, as are most other managerial and office staff, and points out the 'ethnic stratification' that this entails. Also Burg (1990: 38) notes the prevalence of Russians in elite positions in the economic institutions of the non-Russian territories.

Returning to our discussion of the Kola Peninsula and the Sámi, one Sámi woman from Lovozero stated that:

> here during that period, and maybe even today, inside Lovozero there is a small, how shall I put it? – well, thing, between people: like, 'you're Sámi, and I'm Komi. We Komi are more civilized, better. And you're Sámi – a dirty person.'

Yet we should not exaggerate the tension between the Sámi and Komi. Although it is an enduring theme in social interaction in the villages and certain individuals take it to great lengths, it is no longer a major issue. Indeed, many of the Sámi and Komi even officially trace part of their ancestry to the other group, not to mention the Nenets and the multitude of identities that constitute the 'Russian' category. This intermingling functions as a damper to bellicosity (Kotov 1987: 11–12). For some interviews reflecting this, see Appendix 4.

Still, during the Soviet era, Sámi identity was the ethnic identity facing the most pressure on the Kola Peninsula. Many children with one Sámi parent chose to register themselves as another nationality when they reached the age of sixteen and were issued their first passport. For example, in mixed marriages with Komi, most children would choose Komi as their passport nationality (Konakov, Kotov and Rochev 1984: 27–29). A Sámi woman from Lovozero also explained that sometimes 'Sámi names were changed into Russian ones'. Yet some factors counteracted this shift away from Sámi identity, such as the quotas for Sámi at institutions of higher education. This arrangement had several aspects that served the Sámi interest: it strengthened their identity by recognizing the Sámi as a group possessing certain rights, it made higher education available to those who identified themselves as Sámi, and it probably served to make some ambitious youths register as Sámi, people who might perhaps otherwise have felt it necessary to discard their official 'Sáminess'. As we shall see in Chapter 5, with the increased attention, funds and travel opportunities that came to the Russian Sámi after 1989, inevitably at least a partial shift occurred away from the former negative status (Beach 1992: 117; Sarv 1996: 138). Nonetheless, pressure has remained against Sámi identity.

To sum up, since the Soviet period, the development at the individual level has leaned towards greater complexity for the category 'Sámi'. Further impetus has come from the fact that the nationality rubric in Soviet passports was discontinued as a part of a more sweeping passport reform, planned since 1990 and implemented in October 1997 (Simonsen 1999). Several Republics of the Russian Federation reacted negatively to the reform, among them Tatarstan, Bashkortostan, Dagestan and Ingushetia (Simonsen 1999: 1075, 1076). Their protests resulted in a compromise whereby they were allowed to insert a separate sheet stating the nationality of the passport holder, but only at his or her request. The Lovozero District's administration also, for a while at least, gave people the opportunity to register the nationality of their children at birth, on their own initiative. (For more on interethnic relations and the complexity of identity, see Appendices 4 and 7 respectively. In the latter, statements from two people protesting against the loss of the nationality rubric in Russian passports are included.)

The Northern Peoples of Russia

The Russian Sámi were one of the twenty-six official northern indigenous peoples under the Soviet system. The concept of these 'Small Peoples of the North' was introduced into Soviet legislation by decrees in 1925 and 1926 (Vakhtin 1994: 31; Kiselev and Kiseleva 1979a: 20). (For various alternative appellations, see Slezkine 1994: 1; Schindler 1992: 53.) In modern usage, they are more often known as 'Indigenous Small-Numbered Peoples of the North' (*malochislennye korennye narody severa*). For the sake of simplicity, we refer to them as 'Northern Peoples'.

The specific Russian term *narodnost* applied in several of the Russian versions of the appellation 'Northern Peoples' denotes a small ethnic group without an industrialized economy or a literature of its own (Szynkiewicz 1990: 2). The Soviet approach to nations and nationalism was narrowly evolutionist, positing various types of ethnic community corresponding to successive stages in the development of the modern nation (Coakley 1992: 4; Calhoun 1997: 99), including *narodnost*, characteristic of the slave-owning and feudal periods; *natsionalnost*, underdeveloped nations; and *natsiya*, fully developed and consolidated nations, characteristic of capitalist and socialist societies (Khazanov 1995: 18; Schindler 1997: 195). 'With the elaboration of Soviet theory of ethnic evolution, *narodnost* came to denote a community situated above the tribe (primitive communism) but below the nation (formed under capitalism)' (Slezkine 1994: 152).

In the mid-1930s, Stalin's approach to nationality issues came to dominate and remained unchallenged. Particularly after the Second World War, this approach slid towards Russian chauvinism, although Stalin himself was from Georgia. In the hierarchy of national evolution, the Russians became the highest and greatest of all nations, followed by the other large European groups in the Soviet Union. The aim for the smaller groups was to become like them: developed and Russian, Russian and developed. Thus, the notion of Northern Peoples like the Sámi was thoroughly entrenched in Soviet evolutionist thinking about nationalities, and official policy towards them reflected these attitudes.

The basis for the category of 'Northern Peoples' was small population numbers; subsistence occupations such as hunting, reindeer herding, fishing and sea-mammal hunting; and distinctive lifestyles (Taksami 1990a: 23). However, a certain arbitrariness existed in the exclusion and inclusion of specific groups within this category (Janhunen 1991: 111; Rybkin 1998: 3). For Vakhtin (1994: 31), the term 'Northern Peoples' is more of a metaphor than a scholarly designation. Nonetheless, certain basic similarities remain among many of the Northern Peoples, not least their treatment as such because of the classification itself.

An important point to note regarding the classification of Northern Peoples is the frequent exclusion of the Komi (along with the Yakut/ Sakha) from the category, because their population numbers exceed the notional 50,000 mark. Although fewer than 2,000 Izhma Komi live on the Kola Peninsula, the Komi as a people number more than 50,000 and have their own republic within the Russian Federation (Tsypanov 1992: 19; see also Appendixes 4 and 7). On the other hand, the Izhma Komi have often been treated as indigenous by the provincial and district administrations and the media on the Kola Peninsula, resulting in some contradictions (see, e.g., Yefremov 1995b: 2).

According to Janhunen (1991: 119–120), the Sámi are in fact only one of between six and ten of Russia's Northern Peoples who live on both sides of the former Soviet borders; others include the Siberian Yupik (Inuit), the Aleut of the Bering Region, the Nanai on the Amur and the Evenks in Transbaikalia. However, the particular power structure of the relationship across the border with a more prosperous country is unique to the Russian Sámi, apart from that of the Siberian Yupik with their cousins in Alaska (see Ainana et al. 1997: 5; Zelensky et al. 1997: 8). The first large delegation of Alaskan Inupiat Inuits visited the settlement Provideniya on the Chukotka Peninsula in 1988, and traffic in both directions has subsequently become frequent.

> The younger generation of [Siberian] Eskimo were astonished to find that their elders could use the Eskimo language to converse fluently with fashionably-dressed American citizens while they themselves were tongue-tied. The following term, the level of attention at compulsory Eskimo language lessons rose significantly. (Vakhtin, related by Vitebsky 1996: 102)

The historical dominance of the Chukchi over the Siberian Inuit was partly undermined because the Chukchi have no relatives in Alaska (Vitebsky 1996: 106), which creates an interesting parallel to the relationship between the Izhma Komi and the Sámi on the Kola Peninsula.

The greatest importance of the other Russian Northern Peoples to the Russian Sámi is that they provide an alternative or additional political dimension and identity to that of the Nordic Sámi, giving them a potentially dual indigenous identity. Several congresses of Northern Peoples have been held, the first ones in 1990 and 1993, both in Moscow and both with active Sámi participation (Sokolova and Yakovlev 1998: 4). The 1990 inaugural conference was attended by Mikhail Gorbachev and Prime Minister Ryzhkov, and the writer Sanghi (of the Nivkh people from southeastern Siberia) was elected president of what later became the Russian Association of Peoples of the North (RAIPON) (Vitebsky 1996: 101). AKS is a member organization of RAIPON, while OOSMO is currently listed as an organization with which the network 'cultivates contacts' (RAIPON 2006). The Russian Sámi activist Anna Prakhova also served as first vice-president of RAIPON for a while.

RAIPON provides a collective voice for the numerically small indigenous peoples of the Russian North; however, the Russian Sámi are among the smaller of its member groups and therefore have more difficulty in getting heard and represented within RAIPON than they do within the pan-Sámi movement.

Claims to Indigenousness

It is sometimes stated explicitly or argued implicitly that the Komi, Nenets or Pomors should be accorded some form of indigenous status (Krupnik 1993: 4; Rybkin 1998: 2). Such demands have been put forward especially in connection with claims for subsidies and fishing and hunting rights, an area where Soviet practice was not always consistent.

The Komi and Nenets on the Kola Peninsula are often referred to as 'indigenous' by the provincial authorities and the media, without further explanation (e.g., Yefremov 1995b: 2); they themselves also occasionally argue for this. One academic statement supporting an approach to indigenousness that would include Komi persons was made by Konstantinov (1999: 1, 14, 16), who argues against focusing on ethnic divisions and instead favours seeing what he terms the 'local tundra-connected population' as a whole.

However, many of our Russian Sámi interviewees were against extending indigenous status to other groups. They consider their historical status as the 'first nation' to be an important part of being indigenous. One of our Sámi informants formulated this as follows:

> Before, there were only Sámi on the Kola Peninsula, there were really few Russians, just a few on the coast, and here [in the interior] there were no Russians, just Sámi. Then the [Komi] Izhemtsy arrived ... The villages became Izhemtsy, while before they had only been Sámi. It's indigenous Sámi land.

According to this perspective, both the Komi immigration and subsequent 'Russian' arrivals are threats to the existence of the Sámi. As a Sámi from one of the smaller villages with a large Komi population said: 'The Komi have their own land, their own Republic ... the Komi Soviet Socialist Republic [*sic*] – and *this* is Sámi land.' Thus, the arguments used against granting the non-Sámi 'Northern People' populations of the Kola indigenous status are that they are fairly recent arrivals, they have their own indigenous land elsewhere, and these groups are not as small as the Sámi. A Sámi woman from Revda explained that the Komi and Nenets:

> ... are newcomers. They aren't indigenous here. The Komi have Syktyvkar where the Komi Republic is, and the Nenets have the Yamalo-Nenets *okrug* [autonomous area], so they aren't indigenous peoples. And therefore naturally the Sámi have priority, because they are the indigenous inhabitants here, and the others are just not very numerous, but that's it. Naturally, if, like, the Sámi should have some privileges and the Komi not, then at the same time, well if you don't like it, then go to the Komi Republic. There you will be equal to the Komi, but here – I beg your pardon – but this is the land of the Sámi and of course the Sámi will have priority.

It is not our intention here to adjudicate between the various claims to indigenousness, but simply to establish the fact for the reader that it often remains undetermined exactly who belongs to which ethnic group on the Kola Peninsula, and which ethnic group(s) can or cannot assert indigenous rights there. Due to mixed marriages and assimilation, locals often see some flexibility or even randomness in the old passport categories and other individual claims to ethnic authenticity and group membership. In any case, we find that Russian 'Sáminess' is one element in an identity landscape that is rich and complex, even containing several ethnic identity options that may entail some form of 'indigenousness'. A long period of intercultural contact and assimilation efforts has also led to the 'everyday culture' (behaviour and practice on a day-to-day basis) of people who identify themselves as Komi, 'Russians' or Sámi, being rather similar despite the different ethnonyms. Most of them use the same language (i.e., Russian), participate in the same economic activities, listen to the same music, watch the movies of the mainstream culture, and so on. For many people, it is only on special occasions, such as cultural events and ethnopolitical meetings, that the specifically ethnic aspects of their identity are enacted. This situation is something the Russian Sámi share with many ethnic minority populations throughout the world.

Notes

1. Kalstad specifically mentions the Yona area of Kovdor, whereas the official document *Poryadok predostavleniya subsidiy iz oblastnogo byudzheta obshchinam korennykh malochislennykh narodov Severa Murmanskoy oblasti (Utverzhdyon postanovleniyem Pravitel'stva Murmanskoy oblasti Ot 26.11.2009g No 540-PP)* specifies the entire Kovdor District as part of the official 'districts of traditional inhabitance' of the Sámi.
2. Note that the full number of registered voters in Sámi in Finland is 9,350, but many of these are below the age of eighteen and thus not actually eligible to vote. In Norway and Sweden, persons under voting age cannot register.
3. Finnmark County and certain municipalities in the counties of Troms, Nordland, Nord- and Sør-Trøndelag, and Hedmark.

4. Both Moscow and St. Petersburg are 'federal cities', surrounded by provinces called Moscow and Leningrad, respectively. 'Moscow' here refers to the federal city and not the surrounding province. These data are from the 2002 census.

CHAPTER 3

LOST LAND, BROKEN CULTURE?

The Pre-revolutionary Kola Sámi

Life in the Siyt

Until the beginning of the twentieth century, the main organizational unit in Russian Sámi society was the *siyt*, which often corresponded to the *pogost*, an old Russian administrative unit (see Utvik 1985: 1; Konstanti-nov 1997: 17). The East Sámi *siyts* are defined as having four main char-acteristics in common: a specific territory with a shared winter settlement (*tallv siyt*) for its members; diverse social ties among the members, includ-ing cooperation and mutual aid; a degree of self-government, including redistribution of natural resources among families; a common cult and cer-emonies (Kuropyatnik 1992: 163; Zorgdrager 1984: 13). Summer camp-sites were numerous and frequently separate for different families from the same *siyt* (Volkov 1946/1996: 37). A *siyt*'s territory would often include salmon rivers, lakes for freshwater fishing, hunting grounds, various rein-deer pastures and in many cases a coastal tract. Most of the Sámi used to lead a semi-nomadic lifestyle, migrating back and forth between their vari-ous means of subsistence according to the seasons (Kiseleva 1994: 72).

Hansen (2004: 374–375) defined the *siida* (the North Sámi equivalent of the *siyt*) as a:

> Sámi resource exploitation collective [*bruksfellesskap*], consisting of several families or households that cooperate on the exploitation of a common area for migration, trapping or other resource gathering … in spring and summer the individual units [families, households] operated separately from one another … whereas in the fall and winter the members would gather in common settlements to engage in collec-tive hunting … and other common activities… .

Bjørklund (1994: 72) further describes this form of organization as 'a way to mediate the carrying capacity of an area'.

The *tallv siyt* was the focal point for the social and economic life of all the *siyt* (Hirsti 1974: 45, 46). In contrast to the later sedentary villages established during the Soviet period, the *tallv siyt*'s location was determined by the availability of lichen and firewood as well as the distance to the various types of land it exploited. The *tallv siyt* was particularly important in the western part of the Kola Peninsula, as it was the only place where the entire *siyt* would gather in the course of the annual cycle. But it was also important in the eastern part: the summer months were filled with intensive work, so the winter months in the *tallv siyt* were the main opportunity for marrying, solving disputes and engaging in trade.

As reflected by the names of the months in the old calendar and the importance of the *tallv siyt*, the variation between the means of subsistence in the different seasons structured Sámi society and culture. It has even been claimed that the difference between the summer and winter activities was so great that one could speak of 'distinctive summer and winter cultures' (Terebikhin 1993: 185). This temporal division of labour was further dissected by a gendered division of labour, although – according to Dallmann (1997: 17) – this was not particularly strong among the Russian Sámi. When the men were not occupied with herding, they would work at many tasks otherwise done mainly by women (e.g., sewing) while women in turn could bring food and other amenities to the men when they were herding, although they did not participate in the actual herding (Terebikhin 1993: 186). This division of labour should be borne in mind when we examine how life was affected by Soviet policy in the next section.

The 1800s: Reform and Immigration

The century that preceded the Russian Revolution saw two big changes for the Kola Sámi. Under Tsar Aleksandr II (1855–1881), colonization of the peninsula was initially supported, while according to Kalstad (2009: 21) reforms were also made that led to what he has called 'the first Sámi Parliament'. A *volost*, an administrative unit, was established for the Sámi of the Kola in 1866 and may have started functioning as early as 1868. This *volost* was formally called the Kolsko-Laparskaya *volost* (i.e., the 'Kola Lapp district'),[1] and was part of the Aleksandrovsk *uyezd*, which again was under Arkhangelsk *guberniya*. According to Kalstad (2009: 22–28), once every year a council of Sámi representatives from the constituencies of Pechenga, Ekostrov, Voronye and Ponoy would meet with a representative of the Tsar in the so-called *Koladak sobbar* or *Kuelnegknyarkk sobbar* – the Kola Congress or Kola Peninsula Congress. Tanner (1929: 332–338) also discusses this system.

It is unknown how these structures of representation functioned in practice. They were neither preserved nor built upon after the Russian Revolution; indeed, they were not even something the Kola Sámi generally remembered before Kalstad once again shed light upon them. However, during the 2000s, the notion of a Sámi Parliament of sorts having existed earlier on the Kola Peninsula has given some impetus to the NGO-based campaign for establishing a Russian Sámi Parliament. The Kola Sámi Assembly – the elected forum that currently struggles to be recognized as Russian Sámi spokespersons by the provincial authorities – is indeed called precisely the *Kuellnegk nyoark sam' sobbar* in Kildin Sámi (Berg-Nordlie 2011b: 58, 70–71).

Meanwhile, the 1800s brought another great change to the Kola Peninsula, which dramatically shaped the future of the Kola Sámi. The increasing immigration of 'Russians' to the Kola Peninsula focused primarily on coastal areas and did not pose an immediate obstacle to the Russian Sámi lifestyle, which has been more deeply based on reindeer herding than the culture of their Nordic kin. Of greater consequence was the arrival of the Komi from the 1880s, since they aimed for the heartland of the peninsula, where the Sámi *tallv siyt*s were situated and where the 'Russians' had made little impact. The Komi came to play a particularly important role for the Sámi in the twentieth century in terms of livelihoods as well as identity.

In 1887, the first four Izhma Komi families moved to Lovozero.[2] The migration of these people to the Kola Peninsula is often attributed to plagues among their reindeer herds in the Izhma area (e.g., Kiselev 1994a: 4). Although this may have been the direct trigger, it seems that the underlying cause was rapid population growth in the Izhma region in the mid-nineteenth century.[3] With the population expanding, people no longer had enough space to continue practising their extensive land use, so out-migration became necessary (Konakov, Kotov and Rochev 1984: 3). In addition to the Kola Peninsula, the Izhma Komi also went to what are now the Nenets autonomous *okrug* and the Yamal-Nenets and Khanty-Mansi autonomous *okrug*s, where their descendants still live. According to the 2002 Census there were a total of 293,406 Komi in the Russian Federation, of which 15,607 were Izhma Komi. A group of 1,128 Izhma Komi lived in Murmansk *oblast*, and 12,689 in the Komi Republic.

The Komi had heard about the good conditions on the Kola Peninsula from labour migrants in the Murmansk fisheries; a few years before they arrived, they sent scouts to check that the area was suitable for reindeer herding (Konakov, Kotov and Rochev 1984: 6, 8). After the 1880s, the Komi continued coming until sometime in the 1930s (Konakov, Kotov and Rochev 1984: 10), and a few possibly came later as well.

The Izhma Komi culture had developed from a fusion of Russian, Nenets and Komi elements in the Izhma region, and the Komi herding system had developed largely by assimilating and transforming Nenets practices

(Fryer 1998: 12; Kotov 1987: 10; Hallström 1911: 278–279, 295; Zherebtsov 1992: 20). The result, as early as the beginning of the nineteenth century, was large-scale reindeer-herding operations for the open market rather than subsistence, and the use of profits to pay hired labour (Konakov, Kotov and Rochev 1984: 15; Krupnik 1993: 177). In contrast, Sámi reindeer herding on the Kola Peninsula was slanted towards subsistence (Konakov, Kotov and Rochev 1984: 18; Volkov 1946/1996: 19). The Kola Sámi were rapidly influenced by Komi reindeer-herding practices, which 'undermined the formerly conservative attitudes of Nenets and Sámi to their herds' (Krupnik 1993: 177). By the late 1800s, the Russian Sámi had adopted many aspects of the Komi system (Krupnik 1993: 175).

The Sovietization of the Sámi

The New Regime

From the Russian Revolution until the collapse of the Soviet Union, the Sámi and the other twenty-six groups officially recognized by the Soviet authorities as Northern Peoples were subjected to various policies aimed at developing their culture and economy according to so-called socialist principles. They were deemed to have been particularly oppressed under the Russian Empire, and their culture was judged to be especially in need of 'modernization' (Slezkine 1994: 143–144). Thus their development warranted extra attention and assistance, so that they might catch up with the 'advanced nations' of the Soviet Union. In the words of the de facto head of the Committee of the North:

> If the whole of the USSR, in the words of comrade Stalin, needs ten years to run the course of development that took Western Europe fifty to a hundred years, then the small peoples of the north, in order to catch up with the advanced nations of the USSR, must, during the same ten years, cover the road of development that took the Russian people one thousand years to cover, for even one thousand years ago the cultural level of the Kievan Rus was higher than that of the present-day small peoples of the north. (Skachko 1931: 20, quoted in Slezkine 1994: 220)

However, the authorities failed to establish a body that could formulate the details of how to make this great leap forward (Schindler 1992: 58). The task was handed from institution to institution, with each institution taking a different angle, without the envisioned 'leap' ever being completed (see Slezkine 1994: 152; Uvachan 1990: 41; Vitebsky 1996: 109; Osherenko et al. 1997: 32). Common to all these policy-making bodies was that they were hardly ever staffed by representatives of the Northern Peoples themselves.

Soviet Inter-war Reforms: Production Nomadism, Collectivization and Repression

The most important initial aspects of the general Northern Peoples policy for the Sámi were collectivization and the replacement of 'nomadism as a way of life' with 'production nomadism' (Kuoljok 1985: 126; Slezkine 1994: 341; Vitebsky 1992: 223). The thrust of this reorganization was to get the reindeer herders to work in shifts in specialized 'brigades' out on the tundra while the women stayed in the villages with the children and elderly to engage in 'gainful' salaried employment. Thus, many men continued to herd reindeer and fish, moving around the tundra according to the seasons as they had done before.

Some such brigades continued living in tents part of the year, while others were provided with wooden huts in places of particular importance and road access. Their activities were modernized in some ways through the introduction of new technology like snowmobiles, radios and helicopters, but their life and work continued to revolve around the old Sámi calendar in much the same way as before. In contrast, the women were increasingly restricted to the village sphere, which became increasingly Sovietized. Thus, Soviet policy resulted in the restructuring of the seasonal, migratory and gender division of labour among the Sámi and came to define the social structure out of which the independent ethno-political organizations were to emanate during perestroika.

Compared to other Northern Peoples, the Russian Sámi are one of the groups among whom 'production nomadism' is thought to have been developed most fully (Kuoljok 1985: 127). This must be borne in mind when we go on to examine its consequences, especially in comparison to the other Northern Peoples.

In Soviet theory, the subsistence economy was seen as embodying an internal contradiction 'between reindeer breeding and hunting in the tundra, and reindeer breeding and fishing in the taiga' (Slezkine 1994: 204). The subsistence economy was ineffective because it stretched the sparse 'forager' labour across vast expanses and diverging activities. The series of central Soviet organs responsible for the Northern Peoples saw it as their task to help the people overcome such irrational arrangements by reorganizing them into progressively larger units, where they would work in specialized brigades dedicated to single economic pursuits (Slezkine 1994: 205; Kuoljok 1985: 119; Vitebsky 1992: 223).

In the very first stage of collectivization, small groups of workers called *artels* were the main collective units (for varying and partly contradictory definitions of *artels*, see Kuoljok 1985: 109; Kiseljov and Kiseljova 1981: 27; Schindler 1992: 56). The initial years after the Revolution were characterized by pressure on the owners of large herds to join the collectives and attempts to persuade the nomadic Sámi to settle down around them. The impact of these developments on the lives of the Sámi was limited, as most continued to work within kin-based structures that corresponded to the old Sámi *siyt*s. However, in 1929, the Sámi of the Kildinskiy *pogost* (an old low-level administrative unit, here corresponding to a village or *siyt*) were removed in connection with the construction of the October Railway from Leningrad to Murmansk – a harbinger of events to come. The Kildinskiy Sámi were relocated, with the largest group founding the new village of Chudzyavr in the mountains about 45 km from Lake Lovozero (Antonova 1988/1996: 171).

In the 1930s, the *artels* were replaced by *kolkhoz*es, which numbered fourteen on the peninsula by 1934 (Kiseleva 1994: 74).[4] This second stage of collectivization was aided by the intensified persecution of 'bourgeois elements' – in most cases, individuals who owned many reindeer or those who stood out from the rest of the community in some other way, such as through contact with foreigners. In addition to 'rationalizing' the subsistence economy, collectivization was clearly intended to eradicate injustices between the poor and the rich: the owners of the means of production and the dispossessed. Among reindeer-herding peoples, the most easily measured unit of wealth was reindeer. If *kulak*s in the rest of the USSR were people who owned land and engaged in production for the open market, then among the reindeer herders they were those who had larger herds. Meanwhile, those who had few or no reindeer of their own were the 'poor men'. The collectivization of reindeer herding on the Kola Peninsula was supposedly a case of 'bitter class warfare ... in which almost all reindeer herders – Sámi, Komi and Nenets – participated, and in every inhabited place there existed two poles – rich and poor, between whom war raged' (Kiselev and Kiseleva 1979a: 60–61).

When the Stalinist purges came to Sápmi, it did not pay off to belong to a border-transcending minority living close to the Finnish and Norwegian borders. Numbers on arrests and deaths during the repression of the Sámi vary somewhat from source to source. According to Kalstad (2009: 39), 97 Russian Sámi were arrested in the period 1937–38, and 40 found guilty of crimes – mostly counterrevolutionary activities, espionage and anti-Soviet activities. Meanwhile, Rantala (quoted in Mustonen and Mustonen 2011: 91) asserts that 111 Sámi were arrested, of which 45 were executed, three died in prison and three never resurfaced.

Particular individuals who drew attention to themselves were also selected for punishment. The most well-known individual case in the repression of the Sámi is that against the non-Sámi scientist Vasiliy Alymov and his mostly Sámi 'co-conspirators'. Alymov was well known for his work on the Russian Sámi and for his close ties to them. In 1938, he was accused of being the head of a secret Sámi nationalist organization and of aiming to become the prime minister of a Sámi Republic, with his colleague Salaskin as the minister of defence. The organization supposedly had between 40 and 50 members. In all, 15 people from Lovozero were executed along with Alymov, and 13 were sent to camps, including Komi, Nenets and Russians, although for obvious reasons the majority were Sámi (Larsson-Kalvemo 1995: 33; Kalstad 2009: 42; Mustonen and Mustonen 2011: 93).

Apart from extreme cases like that of Alymov and his supposed co-conspirators, milder forms of prominence – like success in reindeer herding – were often sufficient to get people into trouble. The persecution of successful reindeer herders struck at the very heart of herder society. This was a society based on the efforts and successes of individual herders and families in building up large herds, with assistance from relatives, young trainee herders and wage labour paid in kind. The removal of those who were most successful also meant the removal of those who were most talented. Although it may be that an especially large percentage of Komi were categorized as *kulak*s due to their larger herds (see Kiselev and Kiseleva 1979a, 63; Kiselev 1994d: 3), many Sámi were also included in their number, and the slant of the persecution undermined the main avenue to pride and respect for Sámi men: successful reindeer herding.

Post-Second World War Reforms: Amalgamation and Forced Resettlement

The years following the Second World War through the late 1950s are referred to by Kalstad (2009: 43–44) as 'the quiet years'. However, this period of relative stability was followed by what he calls 'the hard years', which lasted until what he refers to as 'the period of cultural revitalization' (Kalstad 2009: 45–49). Soviet policy regained its vigour and ambition, and in 1957 a decree was issued concerning 'means for the further development of the economy and culture of the Northern Peoples', recommending the intensification and enlargement of industrial and agricultural projects related to them (Kiseleva 1994: 75; Slezkine 1994: 339). What followed for the Sámi was the policy of *ukrupneniye*, in which the *kolkhozes* were fused into greater *sovkhozes* (*sovetskoye khozyaystvo* – Soviet farm, state farm) (Vitebsky 1992: 232).

In addition to reflecting Khrushchev's theory of agriculture, *ukrupneniye* made room for military expansion on the geo-strategically crucial Kola Peninsula (Konstantinov 1996: 60; Sarv 1996: 137; Lazarev and Patsija 1991: 203). In comparison to the former *kolkhozes*, the *sovkhozes* were larger, more industrial and mechanized; they relied on more varied economic activities and were 'state-owned enterprises run by appointed officials and salaried employees' (Slezkine 1994: 212; see also Konstantinov 1997: 17). In the *kolkhozes* the employees had been paid according to the profits of their *kolkhoz*, and they were freer to handle the funds of the *kolkhoz* and determine their own working hours (Beach 1992: 119). Meanwhile, in the *sovkhozes*, the state guaranteed their income, but also exercised greater control – increasingly through non-Sámi management personnel.

In connection with the replacement of the *kolkhozes* by *sovkhozes*, eleven predominantly Sámi villages were subjected to 'liquidation' and the inhabitants transferred to four large *sovkhoz* villages, where they became an ethnic minority.[5] Thus, in 1959, the residents of Chudzyavr (originally from Kildinskiy) were moved to Lovozero. The land around the village of Koarrdegk (Voronye) was flooded for hydroelectric production, and most of the inhabitants were moved to Lovozero in 1965. The people from the villages of Varzino and Drozdovka were resettled in Lovozero over a period of four years, and those from Chalmne-Varre/Ivanovka were moved to Krasnoshchelye. Later, the inhabitants of a coastal village were also resettled in Lovozero (Sarv 1996: 137). Those who were resettled were given little or no prior warning. Moreover, the funds transferred to the local authorities to cover the cost of relocation were not made available to the people, resulting in considerable hardship (Antonova 1988/1996: 171). They had been promised that new housing would be available when they arrived in their new places of residence, but in practice that was seldom the case. By 1991, these old pledges had still not been fulfilled, and some of the families concerned again raised the issue (Kuznetsova 1991: 2).

During the heyday of the perestroika reforms, one Lovozero Sámi wrote to the local newspaper *Lovozerskaya pravda* about her memories of when the people from the small village of Varzino had come to Lovozero. Her family of three had been living in one flat with two small rooms and a kitchen until the new people arrived. They had to make room for three Varzino families, consisting of eleven people, bringing the total number of people in the small flat up to sixteen. It took five years before anyone was able to move out (Vatonena 1989: 89). Another Sámi, who was among those who were moved to Lovozero, remembers how they were lured to the area – and the hard times that followed:

> They simply just tricked people, told them that 'in Lovozero houses have been built for you, people are waiting, the apartments are ready, everything has been prepared.' Some even said that they would play music when they arrived, that they were expecting them, would come out and meet them and invite them in. But when they came here, it turned out that neither jobs, nor flats nor anything had been prepared. They started looking for places to live themselves. Some had relatives of a kind, and they moved in with them. Those who didn't have relatives just begged somebody, and that way everybody found shelter.

After *ukrupneniye*, Lovozero was the only village that remained 'national', in the sense of officially 'Sámi', although the vast majority of its inhabitants were not Sámi (Slezkine 1994: 340; Vatonena 1994: 32).[6]

National in Form, Socialist in Content

Soviet nationality policy was reflected in Stalin's slogan from a 1930 speech: 'national in form, socialist in content' (Kuoljok 1985: 13; see also Szynkiewicz 1990: 3). According to the idea embedded in this slogan, 'nationality was "form"'. '"National form" was acceptable because there was no such thing as national content' (Slezkine 1994: 142, 387). The peoples united under communism would be allowed to retain their cultures, in 'forms' such as national costume, folklore and language, whereas their economy and social structure were to be made to conform to the standards of communist development.

It was thought that the establishment of the Soviet industrial economy and relations of production would first result in 'flowering' (*rastsvet*), then 'coming together' (*sblizheniye*) and eventually 'merging' (*sliyaniye*) (G. Smith 1996: 5; Blakkisrud 1997: 14; Simonsen 1999: 1070). In the end, all the nationalities and cultures would be fused in the great Soviet melting pot. With regard to the Sámi, the aim of *sliyaniye* was in many ways achieved. They retained their nominal ethnic identity in censuses and passport nationality rubrics, while the majority of them moved increasingly further away from the land-based livelihoods that had previously characterized their lives. Similar developments took place among most of the Northern Peoples. Thus, between 1959 and 1979, the share of the Northern Peoples engaged in land-based economic activities sank from 70 to 43 per cent (Slezkine 1994: 373).

Among the Sámi, as among the Northern Peoples in general, the *internat* (boarding school) had the function of disengaging children from land-based livelihoods. Such schools were first established among the Sámi in the 1920s (Utvik 1985: 52), but were reformed and greatly expanded in the 1950s (Kiselev and Kiseleva 1979a: 127). Russian Sámi children were sent to various boarding schools, but among the most important was the one in Lovozero. Along with the *internat* in Krasnoshchelye, the Lovozero *internat* is the only one still operating in its original form today. According to Slezkine, 'the task of the schools was to turn out little Russians' (Slezkine 1994: 237). In order to become 'Russians', the children had to assimilate a different lifestyle:

> What followed was a cultural revolution of the most basic kind. The native children had to relearn how to eat, sit, sleep, talk, dress, and be sick, as well as to assimilate

a totally new view of the world and their place in it. ... The teachers disliked what they as saw as 'a shopkeeper mentality', 'national prejudice', religious superstition and a lack of discipline. (Slezkine 1994: 241)

An important part of the Sámi 'everyday culture' was food, and this was also an area in which the *internat* had a particularly hard struggle. 'The teachers were bent on acculturating the [Sámi] children; i.e., they were force-fed Russian food, [such as] potatoes and semolina pudding, even though they would have preferred the traditional fish and reindeer meat' (Sarv 1996: 136). A Sámi woman from Lovozero explained how the *internat* disrupted the transfer of culture from parents to children:

It was good that the children were given the opportunity to learn, the parents were happy, but then it turned bad. ... They started to understand, and we started to understand that, when the children started to learn they also forgot their language, they started to forget. The parents live in the tundra, but they live and learn in the Russian schools. ... Before, the parents taught us from the time we were in diapers ... a child grows up seeing that Mummy is sewing, and we'll ask too: 'Mummy, give me the needle, I want to sew'. And then we'll sew what she's sewing, no serious artefacts, but still we'll learn to sew. We didn't start to learn baking bread, but earlier we'd bake bread ourselves out on the tundra ... and the boys didn't learn to make sleds, lassoes. ... Everything's become very difficult. And then we understood what a mistake had been made, the language had also been forgotten. That's the main thing – we forgot the language, we started to forget.

During the second half of the Soviet period, life expectancy dropped as precipitously among the Russian Sámi as it did among the other Northern Peoples, by about twenty years. Between the 1960s and 1980s, the average life expectancy of the Northern Peoples sank to about 45 for men and 55 for women (Slezkine 1994: 375; see also IWGIA 1990: 16). In comparison, the Russian average in 1991 was 64 for men and 74 for women (Zavalko 2011: 201). Among the Sámi, it is possible that the most important reason for this socio-demographic change for the worse was the loss of control over the land on which they had lived and depended for so long, due to Soviet reforms and its appropriation for purposes like the nuclear tests briefly mentioned earlier. In the next section, we look at how the situation of the Sámi did and did not change with the demise of the Soviet state.

The Social Situation in the Wake of the Soviet Collapse

Reindeer and the Russian Sámi

Despite the association many outsiders make between reindeer herding and Sámi culture, the linkage is not at all that close. In Scandinavia, it has been estimated that less than 10 per cent of the Sámi are directly involved in herding (Brantenberg 1985: 27; Beach 1988: 6); and according to official Norwegian statistics (SSB 2009), the total number of Sámi in Norway who are in any way connected to reindeer herding is 3,010. Other economic activities, such as fishing, hunting and gathering, have historically been more important. Correspondingly, large sections of the Nordic Sámi population downplay reindeer herding as a symbol of Sáminess and instead focus on more 'universal' Sámi cultural markers, such as the *yoik* (a traditional singing style) and the wearing of national costume.[7] It could be argued that in the Nordic states reindeer herding is a stronger symbol of Sáminess in the minds of non-Sámi people than for most of the Nordic Sámi.

Similarly, among the Russian Sámi, only a minority is currently engaged in herding, although according to Kalstad (2006: 19), the great majority of Russian Sámi descend from people for whom the reindeer had a fundamental economic relevance. However, on the Kola Peninsula, activities other than reindeer herding were also highly important. Various forms of food gathering, especially picking mushrooms and berries – sometimes referred to as 'the silent hunt' – were of almost universal importance among the Sámi (Beach and Anderson 1992: 221; Volkov 1946/1996). Historically, great geographical and seasonal variations have occurred among the different groups of Sámi; the Lovozero Sámi, for example, lived almost exclusively from fishing in Lake Lovozero (Ushakov and Dashchinskiy 1988: 47).

There can be little doubt as to the great importance of land-based economic activity for the Sámi before the Russian Revolution (Volkov 1946/1996: 28), which is reflected particularly well by the old calendar, where all the titles of months relate to the importance of the land and many of them to the reindeer, even though large-scale reindeer herding gained a prominent place in the economy only as late as the sixteenth century (Zorgdrager 1984: 16) as a result of the combination of population pressure and taxation schemes that led to a depletion of wild reindeer and other game (Beach 1994: 171; Ushakov 1996). In their classic studies of the Russian Sámi, Kharuzin (1890) and Hallström (1911) disagreed about the relative importance of reindeer herding and fishing; Kharuzin emphasized fishing whereas Hallström also accorded reindeer herding great significance (Utvik 1985: 59; Hallström 1911: 246). During the Soviet era, salmon fishing continued to be of great importance to the Sámi. It was reorganized in the brigades of the collective farms. The collective farms in the former Ponoy District, mainly Iskra and Odd-Syit, harvested 59 tonnes of salmon in 1934 and 155 tonnes in 1939 (Kiseljov and Kiseljova 1981: 65). In 1954, more than 100,000 salmon were allegedly caught in the Varzuga River, with a total weight of more than 265 tonnes (NINA 1996: 31). Moving eastwards from salmonless Lovozero to the small, roadless villages of Krasnoshchelye, Kanevka and Sosnovka, we find a noticeable shift towards more salmon-centred subsistence economies. Here salmon is still often served for breakfast, lunch and dinner, on the same day, several days a week. As a Sámi from one of the villages put it, 'there is no way without fish. It's our national dish, and we eat it all sorts of ways: raw, boiled, salted.'

Still, the reindeer have assumed a symbolic power on the Kola Peninsula that far exceeds their contemporary practical – and historical – importance. This symbolic association between the reindeer and the Sámi is also conspicuous in old myths; for example, it has been argued that the meaning of a central Russian Sámi mythological legend *Myandash* is that 'what is good for the reindeer is good for the Sámi' (Robinson and Kassam 1998: 22; see also Kalstad 2009: 62).

The Loss of the Salmon Rivers to Foreign Sports Fishers

With the onset of perestroika, Sámi salmon fishing was in for another shake-up. The *sovkhoz* fishing brigades were cut back, and after a few years of tentative foreign activity on the Kola Peninsula, fishing rights in several of the biggest rivers were leased to foreign companies involved in tourism. Controversies ensued, particularly regarding control over the Ponoy, Varzina, and Lumbovka rivers.

The American company Kola Salmon Marketing initially signed contracts with the heads of the Lovozero District Administration in the early 1990s. When the administration came under new leadership, these contracts were revoked, and conflicting – and less advantageous – ones were signed with the mainly Finnish company Nature Unlimited (Tret'yakov 1998: 5; Yefremov 1998b: 5; Konopatov 1997: 3). An article in the newspaper *Lovozerskaya pravda* insinuated that this income was used by the new administration leadership to purchase real estate in Murmansk for private purposes (Yefremov 1998b: 5). The former district leadership had also transferred the rights to the Lumbovka River to Sámi entrepreneurs.

Such developments clearly demonstrate the general lack of benefits to the indigenous population from salmon tourism. Using their rights to the Lumbovka, the Sámi attempted to enter the salmon tourism business on their own terms, but failed when their Sámi-styled tourist camp was plundered and subsequently torched by the military from the Gremikha submarine base in 1993 (Larsson-Kalvemo 1995: 97). The military had been blocking the access of the salmon to the river by stretching nets across it. After the Sámi removed the nets, the military arrived several times by helicopter to frighten them and confiscate – among other things – their electricity generator (Vatonena 1994: 32).

Both the production of a critical documentary on the issue by Johs Kalvemo for Norwegian Sámi television in 1994 and subsequent support from some Norwegian Sámi failed to revive the Russian Sámi sports-fishing business (Konstantinov 1996: 58, 65–66; Pedersen 1996: 68). Instead, the river was sub-leased to the company Nature Unlimited. The new district leadership then discontinued the district administration's contract with the Sámi entrepreneurs and instead signed a new contract on the Lumbovka River directly with Nature Unlimited. In the final count, the Sámi got little out of the arrangement (Tret'yakov 1998: 5; Yefremov 1998b: 5). Locals complained: 'It's our river after all, but the money, why does it go out to the province somewhere? ... If only 10 per cent of it all, of the whole contract, went to the state, to the village, then it would be felt. But not a single per cent is visible.'

Things subsequently worsened. In 1995, to show once and for all who controlled the rivers and decide to whom they should be let, the new municipal leadership sent policemen wearing black balaclavas and carrying automatic firearms to clear the Kola Salmon Marketing camp on the Varzina River (Alekseyeva 1997: 3; Yefremov 1995a: 2). At the time, the camp was full of wealthy foreigners, so this episode proved unfortunate for the public relations of all parties. A court of international arbitration in Stockholm, the Court of the Lovozero District and a Moscow conference on international mediation all agreed that the district administration should pay nearly one million dollars in compensation to Kola Salmon Marketing; the Lovozero Municipal Court further declared the contract of Nature Unlimited on the Varzina River to be invalid (Tret'yakov 1998: 5; Alekseyeva 1997: 3). Thus, not only did the new municipal leadership manage to sign an illegal deal for more years for less money, of which the locals saw nothing, it also got itself and the inhabitants of the district deeply into debt.

Considering that it cost foreign customers between U.S.$6,000 and U.S.$7,000 a week to go salmon fishing on the Kola Peninsula (Tret'yakov 1998: 5), it was hardly surprising that the locals felt cheated. In their defence, the foreign companies pointed out that they had bought Krasnoshchelye a power saw, boats, gas tanks and snow scooters and had helped with construction; they also claimed that the catch-and-release method they employ is less environmentally damaging than fishing for food (see Andreassen 1998: 3). In Kanevka, they set up a baking oven and helped out with dental care and occasional helicopter transport.

However, for the villagers, this could not compare to the value of the rivers. People from the municipal centre of Lovozero tend to see it as lost profit as a result of unfortunate business deals, but many of the inhabitants of the smaller villages along the rivers are also opposed to foreign tourism in principle since it displaces their own right to fish (Yefremov 1998b: 5;

Luk'yanchenko 1994: 62). To those who actually live on the rivers – in both senses – a lifeline has been severed. Two Sámi neighbours from one of the small, roadless villages along the rivers explained how the very basis of their impoverished village had been taken away:

> – [Neighbour 1:] We have been fishing informally our entire lives. [Now] we're never supposed to fish in that river again, but every day we need to live somehow, don't we? The village was built here for what? To live well and catch fish and so on and so forth, right? So that we would have everything. And suddenly they make a ban. Only recently did they start selling licences, and before that it was illegal to fish at all.

> – [Neighbour 2:] You need to live somehow. So you go and fish, and the next time they catch you, and then you get a fine too.

The foreign companies make the most of the exclusive rights to the rivers that they have paid for. In an advertising video, one company pointed out that 'no one else from the outside world is allowed to fish *our* rivers except our guests. Unlike some Kola rivers, *locals* are not allowed to fish' [italics in original] (Robinson and Kassam 1998: 97–98). Some of our Sámi informants could testify to the veracity of that advertisement: 'If you go poaching further down there where their camp is … they immediately complain to the authorities, and then the inspectors come.' In contrast, the position of the foreign investors was so strong that the fishing camps of Nature Unlimited were reported to be closed to inspection by the authorities of both the Lovozero District and Murmansk Province (Kobelev et al. 1998: 2).

Although the rights of the Russian Sámi to the rivers on the Kola Peninsula were in fact provided for indirectly by presidential decrees, this fact was entirely ignored by the provincial authorities because of the lack of coherence between central and regional authorities in Russia (Jillker 1994a: 18). As a result, the Sámi were left in the same situation as many other Northern Peoples. As Chuner Taksami (1990b: 33) put it in the opening address at the founding conference of the Russian Association of Indigenous Peoples of the North, 'Fishing quotas are as always fixed in Moscow, in ministerial cabinets. They force us to steal the fish, people say. In this way whole peoples become poachers on their own land.' Similarly, a Sámi from Kanevka asked in a letter to a Nordic Sámi magazine, 'why must the locals fish like thieves in their own river, while anything is possible for foreigners?' (Zaharov 1994: 35).

Whether it is Muscovite, Murmanchan or Lovozerets bureaucrats and politicians who are to blame or foreign businessmen and their clientele, perestroika brought another downfall for indigenous fishing.

The Seydozero Nature Reserve Issue

As well as making inroads into resources of great material importance to the Russian Sámi, such as the salmon rivers, perestroika also produced threats to resources of more symbolic value, such as the Seydozero Nature Reserve. (For a discussion of the various levels and concepts of nature reserves, see Yefremov 1997a: 1; 1997b: 3.)

Lake Seydozero is situated in the mountains adjacent to Lake Lovozero. The name 'Seydozero' comes from the Sámi *Seydyavr*, which is a combination of the words 'holy rock' and 'lake'; Seydozero played an important role in the traditional religion of local Sámi (Smirnov 1997; Rykova 1990: 3; Bjørklund and Brantenberg 1981: 69). It is said that there were taboos against going there too often, women bathing in its waters and herding reindeer in its vicinity (Ryzhova 1997: 5; Bol'shakova 1997a: 2). The Sámi would fish there only once a year, and then only in conjunction with special rituals (Belyayev 1988: 4). According to Robinson and Kassam (1998: 77), the greatest shamans were buried on one of the two islands in the lake.

Impressive standing stones are located in its vicinity, as is the Kuyva, a large pattern considered to resemble a human figure on the rock face overlooking it. For the past hundred years, the enigma of Seydozero has attracted numerous scientists from Russian and foreign research institutions, some of whom have reached rather speculative results, scientifically speaking, declaring the Seydozero valley the cradle of civilization and/ or a source of cosmic energy (N. Bogdanov 1997: 3; Galkin 1997b: 5; Bol'shakova 1997b: 5; Bol'shakova 1997d: 5). As if this were not enough to enhance its mystical powers, according to N. Bogdanov (1997: 3), more than thirty documents from Barchenko's in-depth research into the mysteries of Seydozero in the 1920s remained confidential and in the custody of the NKVD/KGB (the Soviet state organs for internal security) after he and everyone who was connected with his expeditions were executed in 1937 and 1938, including the Sámi guides.

The speculations about the ancient civilization of Seydozero are not all that unusual and have parallels in ideas that researchers from the outside have held about the Sámi in earlier times. The group has previously been classified as 'Mongoloid', Finns, the 'root race' of both 'yellow and white races', and the lost tribe of Israel (Beach 1988: 4). Similarly, the Basques have been popular as subjects of historical creativity and have been held to be the survivors of Atlantis, the sole direct descendants of the European Cro-Magnons, immigrants from the Caucasus, immigrants from North Africa and – again – a lost tribe of Israel (Connor 1992: 56). Such theories may gain in-group popularity in times when ethno-politics have increased importance. Thus, a Hungarian scholar sought to demonstrate that the Biblical Adam had been a Magyar (Argyle 1976: 39), and it has been claimed that German was the language spoken in the Garden of Eden and the original Old Testament (Connor 1992: 56).

Modern Sámi ethno-politics are strongly affected by the notion of indigenousness – namely, the local origins of the ethnos and their status as 'firstcomers'. Hence, ethnic mythologies of 'magnificent origins in faraway lands' would be incoherent with the dominant ethno-political discourse, which is based on the ancient presence of the Sámi in Sápmi. Yet the previously mentioned image of Seydozero as an aboriginal place for the whole of humanity fits well into the Sámi historical narrative; in this case, it is not 'we' who have a glorious past in 'another place' (like the Basque 'Atlantids'), it is the rest of humanity which hails from 'our' territories. In its extreme consequence, some of the Seydozero myths carry the implication that the Sámi heartland is an 'Eden' of sorts, a place 'they' left but in which 'we' remain. Some Sámi interviewees did indeed discuss the perceived universal importance of the lake, like this woman from Revda:

> Seydozero – this is the pearl of the Kola Peninsula, it is held to be a sacred lake, and now they're even saying that the Kola Peninsula is the centre of the original homeland of humanity. Hyperborea [Giperboreya] … all of humanity, according to many scientists, came out of the Arctic … this lake is in fact a northern Shambala – do you understand? – that is to say it's a sacred place. That's why I'm telling you it's necessary to preserve this land and take care of it ourselves.

It is probably of importance that the mythology of Seydozero makes it not merely a holy land for the Sámi, but also a place that carries meaning for all of humanity. As such, it is an object of great pride and perhaps also great responsibility.

The Soviet Union also felt a need to preserve the area. The Seydozero Nature Reserve was established in 1982, in conjunction with a wave of new reserves in the Soviet Union, and expanded in 1983 (Yefremov 1997b: 3; Zazulin 1982: 1; Tumka 1983: 1). However, these nature reserves were set up for approximately ten years only, and by 1995 Seydozero had lost its reserve status. Subsequently, the Mountaineering Club of Alpinists and Tourists of the industrial city of Apatity arranged a five-day conference in the summer of 1997, with financial support from a U.S. charity and the industrial management of the mining town of Revda. The conference bore the title 'Khibiny – with one's own eyes' and included visits to the industrial towns around the Khibiny mountain range, although the actual conference proceedings were held on the shores of Seydozero.

The conference resolved to support the inclusion of Seydozero in a new national park under the name 'Khibiny' – despite the fact that Seydozero lies in the Lovozero mountain massif, not the Khibiny mountains (the two are separated by the great Lake Umbozero). Administrative control of this park was to rest with the twin cities of Apatity and Kirovsk, which would provide for the further protection of Seydozero and in turn provide for the development of their tourist industry. When the result of the conference became public knowledge, there was an outcry against transferring Seydozero from Lovozero to Apatity and Kirovsk, which are overwhelmingly populated by 'Russian' industrial workers and other 'newcomers'. The land is seen as 'the national pride of the Sámi' (Galkin 1997a: 2), 'the sacred heartland of the Lovozero Sámi' (Robinson and Kassam 1998: 77), and is not to be given away or sold, and certainly not to the 'Russians' on the other side of the mountains.

For some interviewees, the preservation of Seydozero exemplified the Sámi struggle for ethnic survival. The previously quoted woman from Revda, for example, invoked the conflict when debating the revitalization of the Sámi people, relating it to the concepts of defending 'land' and 'rights', which she again linked to the survival of the Sámi ethnos.

> Russian (*russkaya*) culture is overpowering the Sámi culture ... but then again, in recent times ... there's been an indigenous peoples' wave (*volna korennogo naroda*), they have understood that they can survive only by uniting and defending their rights. ... Maybe because of this the self-appreciation of the Sámi has increased, they've started looking at their culture differently, they've understood that they've got to preserve their ethnos, which means preserving their culture, their land, their economic activities (*khozyaistvo*), their reindeer. They've understood that now there's a wave of rebirth of the Sámi culture. ... And now they want to make Seydozero a national park, but there's some disagreement. Because this is ancient Sámi land.

It is important to note that the Seydozero conflict was also a question of somewhat more 'material' concerns: access and revenues. These worries were also expressed by interviewees, although seamlessly integrated with articulations of the lake's symbolic value, as in the pessimistic predictions of this Lovozero woman:

> We will lose our Lovozero land, they will control it. Instead of us, the Kirovsk people will have it at their disposal. ... And the money [from tourism to Seydozero, etc.] will go out to the Federal Treasury and to Kirovsk and Apatity, that's where it will go. ... And if they decide to throw us something, then good; and if they don't, then we won't get anything. And our land will be lost, the holy land of our ancestors. That is after all where our very-very first ancestors lived, all over the place there. And suddenly that land will be lost. Those places are truly so historically valuable and famous that we should never ever let them out of our hands no matter what. They left them to us, and we should hand them on to the next generation.

The Reindeer-herding Sovkhozes in the 1990s

The Soviet era left two main reindeer-herding *sovkhozes* on the Kola Peninsula: Pamyat Lenina ('In Memory of Lenin') – formally renamed Olenevod ('The Reindeer Herder') but still often colloquially known by its former name – in Krasnoshchelye, and Tundra in Lovozero. Tundra tends to receive the most attention due to its greater size and more accessible location. In 1993, the *sovkhozes* were turned into TOOs – *tovarishchestva s ogranichennoy otvetstvennostyu*, which can be interpreted as 'cooperatives' or 'associations of fellow craftsmen', but are technically limited stock companies in which the management continues to have at least as much power as it did during the Soviet period (Konstantinov 1997: 15; Beach 1994: 182; Luk'yanchenko 1994: 54). The employees, other people in the villages and, in moments of forgetfulness, even members of the administration persist in referring to the TOOs as *sovkhozes*. In many respects, the only thing that seemed to change with perestroika was the name and economic predicament of the institutions. Like former *sovkhozes* across the former Soviet Union, 'they are "icebergs": of different sizes, perhaps melting a little at top and bottom, or maybe growing imperceptibly, floating and jostling one another in an unfriendly sea' (Humphrey 1991: 8). We might also add that the part of them that is visible and melting is only a fraction of the whole. They are 'total institutions' that penetrate much deeper than their nominal economic activities (Humphrey 1995: 7). Some 500 former and current workers at Tundra were issued stocks when it was turned into a TOO. However, only about ninety of the stockholders were reindeer herders, and perhaps seventy of these were Sámi (Konstantinov 1996: 54; Luk'yanchenko 1994: 55; Selivanov 1990: 3). These former *sovkhozes* remain the only institutions that herd reindeer on a large scale.

In 1994, the Swedish–Russian joint venture Norrfrys-Polarica started building up a slaughterhouse to EU standards on the grounds of the former *sovkhoz* Tundra (Sokolova and Yakovlev 1998: 14; Yefremov 1993a: 1; Semisorov 1993: 2), hoping to profit from the export of reindeer meat to the West (World Reindeer Peoples' Union 1997: 13). Starting in 1992, Norrfrys-Polarica bought more than 80 per cent of former *sovkhoz* Tundra's and part of Pamyat Lenina's annual production of reindeer meat (Konstantinov 1996: 57; Kuznetsova 1998: 1), despite numerous conflicts, in particular, overpayment for the meat (Sashenkova 1998f: 2; Antonova and Sashenkova 1998: 1).[8] During the summer of 1998, Tundra and Norrfrys-Polarica signed a new ten-year contract, securing the slaughterhouse as Tundra's property for a U.S.$40,000 loan from Norrfrys-Polarica, to be paid with meat (Yefremov 1998c: 2). According to Konstantinov (2011: 193), Norrfrys was the main buyer of reindeer meat and berries on the Kola Peninsula and a major local employer until recently selling its facilities to a Russian investor and leaving the province, taking its equipment with it.

Compared to the conditions of many other enterprises in the Russian North, Tundra's access to strong foreign capital to replace that of the Soviet state should have been advantageous, but in fact it made little difference to the vast majority of its employees, particularly its reindeer herders. For example, during the first half of 1998, they received between fifty and a hundred roubles each per month (Yefremov 1998c: 1), which is not all that striking in itself as during this period many people in Russia did not receive any wages at all. Yet few other Russian firms received large investments from abroad or enjoyed such easy access to foreign markets. The former *sovkhoz* Tundra was in a better position.

The situation of the herders was basically a continuation of the late Soviet era, with extremely poor living conditions in the tundra, often verging on life-threatening. Both the presence of a strong foreign market for their produce and the election of a Sámi director of Tundra for a period failed to alleviate the hardships of herding; thus, the decline continued in the 1990s. In addition, the herds themselves were under threat from widespread poaching, which increased steadily along with poverty and general lawlessness. One Sámi informant explained:

> the soldiers sit there with no money, the factories sit there with no money and naturally they all go out to the tundra and shoot free meat. Free meat, that's reindeer. So they kill the reindeer, and poaching has reached a terrible level. And our *sovkhoz* Tundra is struggling endlessly because the reindeer are being wiped out.

The management of Tundra claimed that one tenth of its herd was lost to poaching every year, with military personnel held responsible for much of this.[9]

Konstantinov (1996: 62–63; 1999: 30, 31) has argued that some poaching estimates may be exaggerated; he further asserts that contact between the herders and the military is often amicable and of mutual benefit and that some *sovkhoz* employees have themselves in times of need killed deer unofficially for food (see also Hønneland 1997; Hønneland and Jørgensen 1998: 246; 1999). Some herders also argued for the peaceful co-existence and even mutual benefit of reindeer herding and military activities, swapping meat for fuel, transport and supplies (Oresheta 1996: 2; Borovaya 1998: 2). These arguments may be important for the social relations between the herders and the military, and the survival strategies of the herders, but the reindeer-herding community persisted in claiming that large numbers of reindeer are being killed by outsiders in some way or another. Beach cites several ways in which this may take place: illegal poaching, military shooting for sport, military all-terrain vehicles frightening reindeer and frequent car and train collisions, especially for Tundra's Fifth Brigade, which travels across a major road twice a year (1992: 139).

The main benefit of perestroika for the Sámi and their reindeer came from the collapse of Soviet industry. Due to the slowdown in production, the levels of pollution and intrusive activity declined, and the development of new industrial projects was almost brought to a total standstill. This situation did not, however, do much to brighten the future of Russian Sámi reindeer herding or other land-oriented livelihoods. As the 1990s rolled towards a massive economic crisis, the situation of the herders remained as bleak as ever. A documentary film made privately by Vladimir Kuznetsov from Lovozero's local television illustrated how these social problems were experienced at the ground level. In 1993, he filmed a group of reindeer-herding families on a summer visit to old settlements in the tundra. When he filmed the same group again in 1998, five of the ten men in the families had died, all from unnatural causes and all in their 20s or 30s. One had died from radiation-induced leukaemia, another had been shot by poachers, a third had burnt to death and so on. The impact of such events on the families and the community is indeed hard to comprehend.

A different but equally clear illustration was life expectancy among Kola Peninsula herder families: 42.5 years for men and 56 for women (Konstantinov 1996: 55; 1999: 34).[10] This fits in with the general picture among the Northern Peoples, among whom every second death in the 1980s was due to injury, murder or suicide (all often alcohol-related), producing a death rate for the 20–34-year-old age group that was six times above the mean for the Soviet Union (Slezkine 1994: 375; Krupnik and Vakhtin 1997: 237). It has been estimated that in 1990 some 80 per cent of the deaths among male Russian Sámi were due to unnatural causes (Sarv 1996: 138). Moreover, in the five years from 1975 to 1980, out of 102 Russian Sámi deaths, 54 were violent (Sidorin 1991: 2). One of the main causes of the low life expectancy among the Northern Peoples seemed to be alcohol.

Land Loss, Uprooting and Alcoholism

When one of the authors (Overland) was carrying out fieldwork among the reindeer-herding Russian Sámi population in the 1990s, alcohol problems were conspicuous at the everyday level. A Sámi woman attempted to explain why she thought some people were trapped in this kind of behaviour:

> Why is it that way? How did it happen? A person doesn't just drink like that, it means that something is weighing down his spirit. ... Maybe if it all went into their own hands like before, when they had subsistence farming, but now they throw

away the antlers, the furs rot, and whatever else. But all of that could be used. Before, they used to sew all sorts of ornaments. They used absolutely everything, they lived freely, they had everything and that made it easier for them.

Anyone with experience of the vodka and beer culture in the rural Russian North at a time of crisis might question whether alcoholism was really a greater problem among the Sámi than among the rest of the Arctic population. For example, Fryer (1998: 88–89) described endemic drinking problems among the Komi in the Komi Republic. Notwithstanding, many interviewees perceived their own people's situation as worse, as in this explanation from a Sámi woman from Revda:

> The Russians drink too. I'm not saying that it's only the Sámi. … Look at the Russians in Revda; the Russian kids drink because the factory is closed, because there is no work, because you can't earn money for your family. … But all the more the Sámi, who have been torn away from their traditional livelihoods. Now very few become herders, very few. Very few work, for example, sewing slippers, waders or boots, really few. Basically people have almost no work. They gather berries, sell, buy vodka, drink. Catch fish, sell again, and drink.

One of the most powerful demonstrations of the higher rate of alcohol abuse among the Sámi relative to other groups was found in the numbers of patients admitted to the Lovozero hospital and kept under observation for 'alcoholic psychosis'. In 1992, 24 of the patients were Komi, while 77 were Sámi; in 1993, 19 were Komi and 68 were Sámi; and in 1994, 13 were Komi and 58 were Sámi (Kaminsky 1996: 150, 153). These figures were certainly not due to the numerical prevalence of the Sámi as about as many or even more Komi live in the area.[11] There must have been another cause.

Although the drinking problem clearly had something to do with the economic crisis, the widespread feeling was that its roots went deeper. When asked whether they drank because of the economic crisis, one answer given by a Sámi interviewee at the close of the 1990s was:

> No, it's not the crisis, it's not the unemployment. You know, it's a crisis of mental boredom. A person has nothing to do. … People who had work and an all right wages drank too, naturally they drank. Why? Because mentally they didn't work. They didn't have to think about anything, didn't have to solve any problems.

This is a point that many visitors to post-Soviet countries in the immediate wake of the collapse felt applied to many of its citizens: that the work ethic, individual initiative and sense of personal responsibility had been destroyed by their disenfranchisement in the Soviet economic system. However, many Russian Sámi interviewees felt that the severity of their problems was not only due to the diminution of their economic individuality, but because with it their ties to the land had been broken.

According to this view, alcoholism was what filled the divide between the Sámi and the very basis of their culture: their land. Among those who still engaged in land-based activities, especially reindeer herding, the divide was perceived as a gaping hole with which they still had to deal. They depended entirely upon land over which they had minimal political control. If powerful non-Sámi actors wanted to detonate nuclear bombs on it, lease it to wealthy foreigners to fly-fish, mine it or turn it into touristic nature reserves, there was little the Sámi could do, apart from protest. Whether they wrote to the newspapers, contacted provincial authorities or told foreign researchers about it, there was little effect.

The key to understanding the estrangement of the herders lies in the difference between their work and life as it was before and after the forced reorganization of the villages through *ukrupneniye*. As explained by a Sámi woman in Monchegorsk:

> When there were twenty people in a village, ten herders … and they knew that he was the main one who did the work, he would naturally be the elite, and he knew that to them he was the chief. He knew that if he treated the land right he would have the right income. Well, that is, when he knew what he was responsible for, where, what he was, he behaved accordingly. But when they send him to one herd today and another tomorrow, that is, when the chief brigadier decides over his head that 'I don't want you to be with the ninth herd, I'll send you to the seventh, you gave me the wrong look, I don't like you, I'll send you away forever', he stopped being someone who could determine things.

Before *ukrupneniye*, the herders were strong and respected in the Sámi community. Collectivization, *ukrupneniye* and the *sovkhoz* brigade system exacted a heavy toll on that feeling of honour. As noted by Hallström (1911: 59), a Sámi herder who lost his reindeer also lost his social esteem. Those who are old enough can still recall how it used to be:

> I still remember when their status was that of an elite … I was small. To start with, first of all, people have been torn away, as proprietors, from the reindeer, from the land. He [the herder] became simply someone who carried out various tasks. When *ukrupneniye*, governmentalization, was carried out, when a person himself doesn't understand what belongs to him, what he is responsible for, of course he degrades. And with that comes a corresponding attitude towards him. So the policy of *ukrupneniye*, of governmentalization, destroyed reindeer herding.

The supply of alcohol has often been an important aspect of the relationship between imperial states and conquered peoples, including that between the Russian Empire and the Northern Peoples (Slezkine 1994: 164, 268–269). As Janhunen (1991: 112) explains, 'alcoholization is just one aspect of the process known as the lumpenization of the northern peoples'. There were drinking problems among the Russian Sámi before the revolution as well, particularly in connection with Norwegian and Russian traders who came to buy their produce (Utvik 1985: 49; Volkov 1946/1996: 123). Thus, development during the Soviet period could be seen as an extension of the situation prior to the revolution. However, looking back, one elderly Sámi woman claimed that drunkenness was much less of a problem before *ukrupneniye* than afterwards.

> I came to work in Lovozero in 1956, and there was no alcoholism here. There was one granny, and every day she used to dash off … to the shop, and people said 'Oh, there she goes to get her bottle'. … It was only her, and people just laughed at her. But no one could say that she drank hard, it was just noticeable, because she was the only one who went to get a bottle. And then with the transfer of all the villages here, we started getting alcoholism. The last village was transferred in 1964, and around that time it all started.

Involuntary Celibacy and Gender-biased Mixed Marriages

For the herders and those who had been torn away from their land, alcohol was a substance that could fill the holes in their lives. The same woman who told about the little 'granny' explained:

> people arrived at a dead end. They didn't know what to do, how to get themselves out of that situation; there was no work, nothing. So they turned to alcohol, they drank, and there were no problems, they were cheerful, they were well, or they were sad and would cry – but there were no problems as such. And out of that again we got all these bachelors. The Sámi started not marrying.

Here she has indicated the linkage between alcoholism and one of the other great social maladies of the herders: not finding a marriage partner, something also emphasized by soul-searching articles in the local media (see, e.g., Sidorin 1991: 2).

Mixed marriages had for a long time been the main form of assimilation for the Russian Sámi, overcoming the high infant mortality as the main restraint on Sámi population numbers (Alymov 1925: 8–9). At the close of the Soviet era, the overwhelming majority of marriages had been mixed ones (Lobanov 1992: 3). However, the structure of Soviet society and reforms resulted in a strong gender bias in such mixed marriages. According to Konstantinov (1996: 55; 1999: 34), the bachelor rate among the Kola Peninsula reindeer herders was around 70 per cent; according to Lazarev and Patsija (1991: 206), Vatonena (1989: 90), Lobanov (1991: 1; 1992: 3) and Sidorin (1991: 2), at least 60 per cent of all Sámi men of marriageable age in the Lovozero District were unmarried.

It must be reiterated that this is not only a Sámi problem, but one that affects many of the Northern Peoples (see Fondahl 1995: 220). For example, among eighty-two Even[12] reindeer herders studied, Vitebsky found thirty-seven bachelors (1992: 234). In addition, among the Izhma Komi on the Kola Peninsula, the out-marriage of women, usually to the larger cities on the Kola Peninsula, was the main cause of migration (Konakov, Kotov and Rochev 1984: 14).

Comparing this in greater detail with the Evenk, a significant growth occurred in mixed marriages between Evenk women and non-Evenk men whereas the opposite remained a rarity. This is thought to be due to the presence of large numbers of single men of other nationalities, but also the prestige of such marriages among Evenk women and the extent of social problems among Evenk men, such as alcoholism, economic dependency and apathy (Karlov 1991: 11). By the late 1960s, hunting, reindeer herding and fishing had become unprestigious occupations and the men engaged in these activities had difficulty in finding someone to marry. However, the further industrial integration of the North greatly exacerbated the situation (Karlov 1991: 6, 11).

As the local school teachers point out, Sámi boys from herding families also often failed to get higher education; they were often academically weak and disruptive at school and at times failed to finish their basic education. This made it impossible for them to get good jobs later, which in turn served as yet another reason why they failed to marry. As such, reindeer herding had become a 'bad job' for anyone wishing to marry.

As observed by Beach (1992: 124), the World Reindeer Peoples' Union (1997: 26), and Yegorov (1992: 3) and recognized in Soviet publications of the late 1980s (e.g., Arevkova 1988: 100; Plyukhin 1986: 4), there have long been difficulties with recruitment to the herding profession. Similarly, Vitebsky (1989b: 23) notes regarding the Even that, 'due to past policies, the younger generation has grown detached from herding' (see also Vitebsky 1990a: 352). Among the Russian Sámi, the few fifteen-year-olds who were still interested in becoming reindeer herders were often among the academically weakest. 'Fifty years ago, the elders remember, they only took the best to work in reindeer herding, and it was respected. Now it is those who have no hope of other work who go there' (Luk'yanchenko 1994: 57). For their part, the young prospective herders argued that they had little reason to try hard at school since they saw the curriculum as totally irrelevant to reindeer herding, which was what they wanted to do. Vitebsky (1990a: 352) wrote about this phenomenon with regard to other Northern Peoples: 'becoming a herder has become a conscious, almost defiant, choice requiring re-education on the job'; he further (1991: 140) stated that 'there is a striking contrast between the children who appear shy and awkward in school but who are clearly strong and confident in the camps, and capable of meeting any demand put on them...'.

Still, the implementation of production nomadism meant divorcing production from reproduction. In other words, as an integral part of *uk-rupneniye*, it '"tore away with force" family life and cultural and social services from work and production' (Karlov 1991: 8) and resulted in 'a separation of the nomadic men from the village-based women and alienation of the children in the village boarding school from the activities and specialized knowledge of the men' (Vitebsky 1996: 98; similarly, Vitebsky 1992: 232; 1989a: 24; 1991: 139). When Konstantinov (1997: 19) notes the continuity of the *sovkhoz* brigade as a 'kinship-based reinterpretation of the *pogost* form of social organization and economic activity', there is striking truth in this (see also Humphrey 1998: 5). The brigades still did much of what the *pogost*s or *siyt*s used to do, including seasonally migrating, and people sometimes had the same kinship relations. The result is that sons often worked with the same reindeer herds as their fathers and grandfathers (Yushkov 1992: 2). Similarly, Vitebsky (1989a: 214) describes Even reindeer-herding brigades as permanent social groups. Often the brigadiers tried to join together in units of fathers, sons, brothers-in-law, cousins and uncles. Unfortunately, apart from the odd holiday visitor and a few cooks, cleaners and seamstresses, the women are generally not a part of the brigade unit, highlighting an important difference between the *siyt*s and the *sovkhoz*es, which placed definite limitations on the reindeer-herding social groups. Kinship without women is short-lived.

Moreover, alcoholism is as much a consequence as a cause of the reindeer herders' troubles and the severance of production from reproduction. Alcoholism was a consequence and an end-product in the sense that it was the main painkiller for alienation from the reproductive sphere and meaningful life. As a Sámi woman from Murmansk explained:

> the women went out to the amalgamated villages, while the men stayed in the tundra, one on one. And as a person, as an individual, he realizes himself there, alongside the reindeer. … What happens with him in the village is that he falls into a different setting where he can't join in. Inevitably it either leads to hard drinking or something else. Well, that is, somehow he resolves the problem for himself, when he experiences that lack of harmony. Usually he fixes the problem with the aid of vodka. But in the tundra he doesn't need vodka or anything else. There he is in his element, there he is a person. But the woman doesn't see him there, she stays in the village.

For the herders, the main bridge from the tundra's productive sphere back to the village sphere, where the women were, was the roughly four months of annual holiday allocation (Beach 1992: 122; see also Sidorin 1991: 2; Konstantinov 1996: 58). As generous a holiday period as this may appear, the divide between the Soviet village and Sámi tundra was self-reinforcing insofar as the herders were already unable to make use of their time off work to bridge the gap (Yegorov 1992: 3). When they came back 'home' to the villages, they were shy and insecure, they had little meaningful work to do and there was nowhere to keep their all-important herding dogs.

In the alcohol-aided, wifeless slump in which Soviet society left many reindeer herders, suicide became a final 'solution' to alienation for many. According to Fondahl (1995: 216), by the end of the Soviet period, three times as many suicides occurred among the Northern Peoples as among the Russians; the Sámi were no exception. Suicide is the third corner in what one of our interviewees described as a vicious triangle, where the other corners are alcoholism and involuntary celibacy (see Appendix 6). It has a function similar to that of alcohol, insofar as it is rooted in, expresses and 'solves' the alienation, or alternatively, 'the insolubility of the contradictions' faced by the Russian Sámi (Taksami 1990b: 29). The link to *ukrupneniye* and Soviet reforms is shown by the fact that suicides have occurred in approximately one out of every three families who moved away from a liquidated village such as the old Sámi settlement of Varzino (Vatonena 1989: 90).

The Two Poles of Russian Sámi Society

We have seen in this chapter how Soviet policy caused – and the 1990s preserved – a polarization of the Russian Sámi on a continuum between a rural, formally uneducated, alcohol-troubled, male, land-oriented pole on the one hand and a more urban, educated and female pole on the other hand. From the latter group of Russian Sámi sprang the first leaders of their post-Soviet ethno-political movement: the intelligentsia, educated at institutions such as Herzen University[13] in St. Petersburg, mostly female, often married to 'Russians' in the cities. In particular, the women from Herzen University, according to Kalstad (2009: 51–52), played a leading role in pioneering both linguistic work and the initial 'ethno-political mobilization during the time of Gorbachev's perestroika'. This pattern is not unique to the Russian Sámi; rather, it is common among the smaller indigenous peoples of the Russian North and is referred to as the 'gender shift' in the literature (Povoroznyuk, Habeck and Vaté 2010: 2).

It is important to note that these two 'poles' of the Sámi community represent generalized types. It would be highly erroneous to assume that all Russian Sámi men are part of a rural *lumpenproletariat* whereas all the women are urbanized and educated. Unfortunately, negative stereotypes of Russian Sámi men have been prevalent in discourses on the Russian Sámi (Konstantinov 1996: 55). The reader should note that in the period covered here there were also Russian Sámi men who went to St. Petersburg, studied at the prestigious Herzen University and got white-collar jobs. In particular, in the generation that came of age in the 1990s, males pursued higher education – sometimes in other parts of Sápmi – remaining conscious of their own ethnicity and going out into society with a desire to improve the situation of their ethnic heritage. We should also not forget the more prosperous reindeer herders, men who have families for whom they provide well and who are proud of still being in the ancestral trade. These men and their successes are also part of the Russian Sámi story. Still, it is important to tell the story of those who bore the brunt of Russianization and failed Soviet policy; they deserve to be heard and have their situation illuminated. Furthermore, the Russian Sámi as a group is still struggling with the previously discussed social problems; and what affects one part of any given community must also have an effect on that community as a whole.

To sum up, Soviet policy led to an erosion of the Sámi identity and culture on the Kola Peninsula, leaving the indigenous people of the area with many social and economic problems as a new phase of Russian history began. Perestroika and the subsequent instability of the 1990s did little to ameliorate the situation, but rather introduced new factors of insecurity and exploitation. On the other hand, the fall of the Soviet Union did mean that independent ethno-politics now became a possibility, and new ties could be forged with ethnic kin abroad, giving the Sámi two potentially significant weapons for countering new and old threats. However, the problems of the land-based livelihoods remained largely unresolved throughout this initial phase, although the ethno-political organizations did make attempts to secure rights to land and other resources. Another issue that was far less controversial, from the authorities' perspective, and that the early Russian Sámi movement tried to address, was language revival, which is the focus of the next chapter.

Notes

1. For some reason, the Russian term 'Lapp' is here spelled 'lap' instead of the more common 'lop'
2. For discussions of the arrival of the Nenets and relations with the Komi, see L.N. Zherebetsov (1982: 196), Brylyova (1990: 2), Volkov (1946/1996: 123) and Brylyova (1996: 158).
3. For example, between 1829 and 1855, the population of the Ust-Tsilemskii *volost* (district) in the Izhma region increased by 220 per cent (Konakov, Kotov and Rochev 1984: 3).
4. Both of the two most important *kolkhoz*es, Tundra in Lovozero and Imeni V. I. Lenina in Krasnoshchelye, were founded in 1930 (Koneva 1971: 2).
5. The names of the four main reindeer-herding villages (and *sovkhoz*es) after *ukrupneniye* were Lovozero (Tundra), Krasnoshchelye (Pamyat Lenina), Tuloma (Tuloma) and Yona (Yona) (Utvik 1985: 64). Pamyat Lenina had previously been called Imeni V. I. Lenina; it was turned into a *sovkhoz* and changed its name only in 1970 (Koneva 1971: 2).

6. Lovozero has had nothing like a Sámi majority for some time. In 1915, the village had 690 inhabitants, of whom only 167 were Sámi, 493 were Komi and 30 were Nenets (Kiselev and Kiseleva 1979a: 25). By the end of the Soviet period, only 5 per cent of the population in the Sámi national *rayon* of Lovozero were Sámi (Vatonena 1994: 32).

7. Although the national costumes (North Sámi: *gákti*) vary greatly from region to region, they are still sufficiently distinct from the national garb of neighbouring peoples to be identified by people from the Nordic countries as Sámi. However, people from Russia do not necessarily recognize them as specifically Sámi due not only to similarities with traditional clothes worn by other ethnic minorities native to the country, but also to a passing resemblance between certain *gákti* variants and Russian folk costumes. One of the authors (Berg-Nordlie) once took part in a delegation of Norwegian Sámi who visited Murmansk city. Since many in the delegation wore *gáktis*, some locals thought that the delegation was a visiting Russian folk dancing troupe. This little anecdote also says something about the extent to which many people in Murmansk province are unfamiliar with their own area's indigenous culture.

8. The export of natural produce from the Russian Sámi to the Nordic countries is not entirely new. During the 1970s, lingonberries and cloudberries were exported to Scandinavia, and reindeer furs, antlers and meat to Finland (Kiseljov and Kiseljova 1981: 124).

9. According to the provincial Agriculture Committee, between 5,000 and 6,000 reindeer were shot illegally every year, out of a total estimated at about 100,000. Even the Special Police Force had trouble dealing with the poachers (Borovaya 1998: 1, 2).

10. An average life expectancy of 44 years has also given for Russian Sámi men in general (Cherkasskiy 1998: 3), a figure sometimes applied to the entire Russian Sámi population (Fedorov and Sinitskiy 1998: 2). As previously stated, the Russian average in 1991 was 64 for men and 74 for women (Zavalko 2011: 201).

11. In 1999, 1,260 Komi and 900 Sámi lived in Lovozero *rayon* and 745 Komi and 743 Sámi lived in the village of Lovozero (Konstantinov 1999: 12; similarly, Beach 1992b: 116; Kaminsky 1996: 150).

12. The Evens and Evenks are two related but distinct Russian indigenous peoples.

13. *Rossiyskiy gosudarstvennyy pedagogicheskiy universitet imeni A. I. Gertsena* – The Russian State University named after A.I. Gertsen (Herzen).

CHAPTER 4

LANGUAGE REVIVAL

Hanging by a Thread

Kildin Sámi is the most important surviving Sámi language in Russia. It is both the language most widely spoken and the only one that has been subjected to an attempted linguistic revival since perestroika. The other Kola Sámi languages are arguably beyond saving, except perhaps Skolt Sámi, which may survive in Finland (Rießler and Wilbur 2007: 41). Hence, saving Kildin Sámi is the last chance the Kola Sámi have to retain one of their languages. However, all linguists who have been involved in the Kola Sámi language revival seem to be able to agree that saving Kildin will not be easy. The number of speakers dropped precipitously during the last century and is now down to a few hundred individuals (see Appendix 2).

The first part of this chapter examines how and why the usage of Kola Sámi languages has declined, providing a continuation of the central theme of the previous chapter: the effects of Soviet policy on the Russian Sámi. We subsequently move on to the first attempts of activists from the Russian Sámi intelligentsia to resuscitate Kildin Sámi. In Chapter 5, the same members of the intelligentsia will resurface as active participants in Russian Sámi organization-building from 1989 onwards.

Language Lost

Soviet Language Policy: From Liberal Support to Suppression

As we saw in the previous chapter, Soviet and post-Soviet policy led to a loss of land and a social upheaval that created difficult conditions for the land-based aspects of Sámi culture. Reindeer herding was 'mechanized', 'sedentarized' and 'collectivized', but at least it survived. In contrast, the

Sámi language fell victim to an even harsher fate: faced with the increasing presence in their lives of a 'Russian' majority – particularly after the liquidation of the Sámi-majority villages – and the increasing encroachment of a Russian-speaking state on their lives, the Sámi language rapidly lost everyday relevance. Falling into disuse in the public sphere, it soon began to be discouraged in the private sphere as well.

During its initial years, in accordance with Leninist nationality theory, the Soviet regime maintained a positive outlook towards the cultures and languages of the Northern Peoples (Brass 1992: 109; Minogue and Williams 1992: 226). In 1908, only between 0.5 and 1.2 per cent of the Northern Peoples could read and write. The Communist Party saw it as its task to make them literate in their own languages (Kuoljok 1985: 59). To this end, a Department of the Peoples of the North was set up in the Workers' Faculty at Leningrad State University in 1925 and became a faculty in its own right the following year; it was subsequently transferred to the Leningrad Institute of Eastern Languages in 1927. In 1930 it was turned into a separate Institute for the Peoples of the North, and in 1953 it became part of Herzen University (Kuoljok 1985: 63; Slezkine 1994: 221; Vitebsky 1996: 96, 109). The first Russian Sámi teacher was trained there in the late 1920s and started teaching on the Kola Peninsula in 1930. By the early 1930s, more than twenty Sámi were studying at the institute (Kiselev and Kiseleva 1979b: 2; 1979c: 2).

In 1930, the institute completed a four-year project on a Latin-based Unified Northern Alphabet for all of the Northern Peoples and started publishing primers and other textbooks in their languages (Vakhtin 1994: 46; Slezkine 1994: 243). Herzen University lecturer Chernyakov wrote a Sámi ABC (1933) based on this alphabet, and primary schools were set up with Sámi as the language of instruction for the first two years (Bol'shakova 1997c: 3; Sorokazherd'yev 1998: 3). However, as in so many other policy areas, with Stalin's rise to power came a series of shifts in language policy, and by 1936 it was decided that there should be a transition from the Latin to the Cyrillic alphabet. In 1937, a Cyrillic-based alphabet for the Sámi language was published by Endyukovskiy (Patsiya 1974: 4). During the Second World War, most policy related to the Northern Peoples came to a standstill, and when activity resumed there was little room for the indigenous peoples' languages.

Throughout the postwar period and continuing up until 1976, the Sámi language was afforded minimal state support, gradually becoming displaced by Russian, in line with the general switch to Russification in the 1950s (Vitebsky 1996: 97).[1] No Sámi instruction was given, children were discouraged or even forbidden to speak the language at school by some of the teachers, and there were no Sámi publications. Consequently, in the public sphere, no Sámi was spoken or written, which in turn put pressure on the Sámi language in the private sphere. The negative attitude towards the language led many teachers to recommend parents not to teach it to their children (Vakhtin 1997: 166; see also Vitebsky 1996: 97; Fryer 1998: 76). Apart from the teachers' admonitions, the low status of Sámi and its disuse in official affairs served as incentives for parents not to pass it on to their children as well as not to use it themselves. As might be expected, the Sámi language went into steep decline in the Soviet Union. This absence of Sámi language from the public sphere, coupled with the discouragement of using it, was not solely a Soviet phenomenon: indeed, the Soviet situation mirrored Nordic policy towards the Sámi languages. However, it was precisely during these 'hard years' (as this period is called by Kalstad 2009: 45) for the Russian Sámi that the Nordic Sámi drive for cultural revitalization began and the Nordic assimilation policies were discontinued.

Demographic reasons can also help explain why the damage done to the Soviet Sámi languages was deeper than to Sámi languages in the West. Although the Russian Akkala, Kildin, Skolt and Ter Sámi were few in numbers, the internal majority of Finland's, Norway's and Sweden's Sámi population consisted of the relatively large North Sámi sub-group. The North Sámi language area was less vulnerable simply due to the sheer number of speakers. Here we should note that other Sámi sub-groups in the West were not so fortunate. Today, fewer and fewer people speak Ume and Pite Sámi, and Inari and South Sámi also have grave problems. Only a few hundred Skolt Sámi speakers remain in Finland (Magga 2002: 13–16). The Lule Sámi language has fared somewhat better than these other non-North Sámi languages, but its position is far from ideal. Also importantly, North Sámi, the strongest Sámi language, is still classified as 'threatened' by UNESCO (Statkart 2011).

A further factor that served to worsen the conditions for linguistic survival in Russia was that Sámi reindeer herders were collectivized into the same economic units as people who did not speak Sámi at all. Initially, the effects were not that bad. According to a Sámi woman interviewed at TOO Tundra in the autumn of 2009, most herding brigades of the *sovkhoz* (eight out of ten) used to be purely Sámi-speaking. However, gradually other people were mixed in and, according to her, no purely Sámi-speaking brigades were left by 2009. Also according to Scheller's (2011: 86) informants, 'Kildin Sami is no longer used as a working language in reindeer herding ... the working languages in the reindeer herding brigades are probably Russian and Komi today.' As such, the Russian Sámi were deprived of a linguistic 'pocket' that was probably vital for the Nordic Sámi during the worst period of cultural repression. When the language disappeared from most non-nomadic communities (in which the majority of the Sámi lived and still live), it continued to be used in North Sámi semi-nomadic reindeer herding communities. The Soviet Sámi languages were denied this 'language fortress'.

Three Generations of Language Loss

The Russian Sámi dialects declined in line with a three-generation pattern in which the first generation consists of grandparents who have lived during a period (and/or in a place) when the language was widely used and, thus, can understand, speak and perhaps read and write it. The second generation is made up of middle-aged and younger adults, many of whom grew up during the 1950s, when, in the case of the Russian Sámi, Russification reached a peak. Vakhtin (1994: 56) referred to this generation as the 'broken generation' as they grew up in an environment in which the language was spoken by the parents, but emulation was discouraged. Consequently, the second generation in such a three-step process of language loss may have a passive knowledge of the language, but is unable to use it actively. The result is a third generation consisting of children and youth who can for the most part neither express themselves in the language nor understand it.

The boundaries between the generations are not fixed or clear-cut; nor do they correspond entirely to demographic age cohorts. Strong variations often exist in the second generation: some people in this generation may have grown up in homes where the language was spoken actively and are therefore still able to express themselves in it; but, depending on the strictness with which language learning was prevented in the individual homes and communities, other people in the second generation may lack even a passive understanding of their parents' mother tongue – instead knowing merely some key words or phrases. Likewise, the third generation may include individuals who understand and sometimes are even able to speak the language, usually because they have been in particularly close contact with the first generation (i.e., their grandparents). It could be argued that among the Russian Sámi the loss of contact with the land also contributed to language loss, or, more precisely, people were torn away from their traditional land-based society structure, which in turn was associated with the usage of Sámi language. They found themselves transferred to a new social structure: the Soviet system, where the Russian language ruled supreme. An elderly Sámi woman from a small, roadless village recounted how her knowledge of Sámi was linked to the tundra life with her parents and how the *internat* education removed her from that life: 'Before I understood, but now I don't understand [Sámi]. During my childhood, our parents simply spoke, and when we went to the tundra I understood. But then ... they sent us to the *internat*.' The liquidation of Sámi-majority villages also meant that their inhabitants were forcibly resocialized into a sphere where Sámi language was a less functional way of communicating than Russian. This phenomenon is not unique to the Russian Sámi, and Vakhtin (1994: 32; 1997: 163, 165–166) among others has argued similarly about the impact of Sovietization, industrialization and loss of land on the languages of the Northern Peoples of Russia in general.

It is also evident that another side effect of Soviet policy – the mixed marriages biased towards Sámi women and Russian men – further intensified the negative effect on the Sámi language. In a family where Sámi is still spoken to some extent, this can be the final blow. One Sámi woman, when asked whether or not her son spoke Sámi, replied:

> – He was with his grandmother all the time, and she always spoke to him in Sámi. And we had him speaking Sámi.
>
> *– So there is a kind of a connection between the older and the young generation?*
>
> – Yes, yes, yes. For her it's easier to speak Sámi than Russian, and he was with her all day, he understands her better in Sámi. But then my husband comes home. My husband, he speaks Russian, and we all start speaking Russian. My son understands that we are speaking Russian, 'clickety-click' [flicks a switch in his head], and he starts speaking Russian.

Mixed marriages influence the most important link in the reproduction of the language: that between parent and child. An elderly woman from Lovozero explained that 'the very best is when the language is received with the mother's milk. That's the very-very best, but now that doesn't happen here. Because very many … marriages are mixed, and in mixed families they speak Russian.' Because there are fewer and fewer people to speak with, those who know the language also start to forget. An elderly woman from a roadless village who used to speak Sámi with her friend before the latter passed away explained that she still remembered a bit, but less and less as time went by without practice. 'No, I haven't quite forgotten. I am losing it, but I haven't entirely lost my language yet. [The other woman] has passed away; I used to speak a little Sámi with her, so that other people wouldn't understand what we were saying.'

Keeping Sámi as a 'secret language' was common among the first generation, which shows that there were already people within the community who did not understand it. It also underlines the severity of the chasm that separates those who know and those who do not know the language and who usually belong to different age groups. Seen from the other side of the language divide, from the perspective of a second-generation child, there is often a sense of having being excluded from the language. One informant from the second generation remembered how:

> Mum and auntie always spoke Sámi with each other. When I was a child I even started understanding and breaking into their conversations. Of course they taught me only Russian and kept their little secrets to themselves, and when I started interrupting, they stopped communicating in front of me entirely. Because I started

eavesdropping on their conversations, and even joining their conversations, but in Russian of course. When I got interested in some word or other, what it meant, Mum said 'Stop it, I don't have time to speak with you' and that kind of thing.

For those who do not clearly fit into a specific generation in the tree-step pattern mentioned above, for example a young girl who can speak a bit of Sámi, there is a certain de facto pressure towards 'assimilating' into the normal pattern for the third generation – even if others of her generation also want the language of their ancestors to survive. One such girl explained that the pressure came from both the demographic forces that pulled her away from her village to study in the city, and the general decline of the language. When asked whether she spoke Kildin Sámi, she replied, 'only at the everyday level, because I have been living away [from the village] for seven years already. And [back in the village] all the elderly people are dying, and the young basically don't really know the language.'

Language Revival?

The fin de Soviet Sámi Intelligentsia

Between 1937 (Endyukovskiy) and 1971 (Kert), relatively few Soviet publications related to the Sámi language were published (Kuruch 1985: 9; Kuruch, Afanas'yeva and Vinogradova 1995: 178). Kert, Senkevich-Gudkova and a few others wrote articles of varying length on aspects of Skolt, Kildin and Ter Sámi linguistics as well as some encyclopaedia entries on Russian Sámi linguistics during the 1950s and 1960s (e.g., Kert 1966). In addition, Kert published a book on language and folklore in 1961. The only dictionary of East Sámi languages issued during this period was Itkonen's (1958) work on Akkala, Kildin, Ter and Skolt. This was not a dictionary for popular use, but rather one oriented towards scientific linguistic usage; it was also mainly read in Finland (Klaus 1987: 145; Sveum 1988: 41). According to Belyayeva (1991: 20), a general dearth of substantial publications existed relating to any aspect of the Russian Sámi during this period.

In the 1970s, Soviet policy makers recognized that the Sámi language would die out entirely under the current policy and that measures would have to be taken to avoid this (Kuruch 1985: 9). Linguistic research and the teaching of Sámi were given fresh starts, having hibernated since the 'period of language building' was terminated in 1937. Sámi mother-tongue classes were reintroduced at the Lovozero *internat* in 1976, and an initial group for the development of Sámi linguistics and instruction was set up under the leadership of the 'Russian' linguist Rimma Dimitriyevna

Kuruch in the provincial Section for Minority Education (Eek 1984: 240; Kuruch, Afanas'yeva and Vinogradova 1995: 178). This mother-tongue teaching was initially implemented in the form of study circles under the auspices of the Soviet children's organization the Pioneers (Alekseyeva 1981: 4) and might have started as early as 1974 (Yefremov 1998a: 2). Classes subsequently ran from the first grade to the third grade; in the 1990s, the fourth grade was also included. After the language instruction was started up, an ABC was published in 1982 (Antonova), followed by new Cyrillic-based dictionaries in 1985 (Kuruch) and 1986 (Kert).

Several prominent figures in the early Russian Sámi intelligentsia worked with Kuruch. Starting in 1976, this 'author's collective' jointly published a dictionary in 1985, edited by Kuruch, and a series of primary school textbooks. The linguist milieu not only constituted the driving force behind the attempt at a long-needed language revival, but it also served as the source from which the first post-Soviet Russian Sámi political leadership sprang. This was the 'core group' of the early post-Soviet Sámi ethnopolitical revival. Judging from both public opinion and the lists of authors in the various publications of the core group, it consisted of between five and ten individuals. Three of the most central participants were Rimma Kuruch, Nina Afanasyeva[2] and Aleksandra Antonova. Characteristic of the Sámi intelligentsia, the core group was female-dominated, and both of the two main Sámi members of the group, Afanasyeva and Antonova, had earned their degrees from Herzen University in Leningrad (Alekseyeva 1981: 4). For most of the 1990s, this core group led the Russian Sámi political movement. Afanasyeva and Kuruch became co-vice presidents of the Association of Kola Sámi (AKS) when it was launched in 1989, and Afanasyeva went on to become its president. Thus, they play prominent roles in the discussion of the Russian Sámi leadership (see Chapter 6).

However, internal disagreements soon emerged within the intelligentsia, as is wont to happen in any intellectual milieu. The disagreements were particularly strong between Kuruch and Afanasyeva on the one hand and Antonova on the other. Whereas Kuruch and Afanasyeva lived in Murmansk city, Antonova lived in Lovozero and hence had a closer connection to the language teachers there. Within the already very small circle of linguists and other activists fighting to revitalize the Sámi language, a split had now occurred. These internal factions within the core group consisted of a minority associated with Lovozero led by Antonova and the majority Kuruch-Afanasyeva group. The latter is named after the two central activists in the core group, who spearheaded the work of the majority faction. A central argument of the smaller Lovozero group was that they felt they had closer links to practical language instruction as well as to the people who were to be taught the language. In 1992, Antonova wrote to the Norwegian Sámi newspaper *Ságat,* accusing Kuruch's methods of causing direct damage to the linguistic revival, saying that she 'came here from outside and took the language of the Sámi from them. She insisted on her own educational approach...' (Antonova 1992). Here, Antonova was referring to a conflict over orthography and alphabets – a conflict which, as seems clear from Antonova's choice of words, had by that time become quite hostile.

Linguistic Rebirth with Complications

In the 1980s, the Kuruch-Afanasyeva group, supported by the Russian Academy of Sciences, focused their efforts on developing a new Cyrillic orthography and alphabet for the Sámi language instruction at the primary school level. They ended up arguing for an orthographic system aimed at reflecting the pronunciation of Sámi words as accurately as possible, including words borrowed from Russian. For example, the words for January and February in Russian are *yanvar* and *fevral* which became *yanvarr* and *fevrall* in Sámi. The Russian *flot* (navy) became *floht* in Sámi, *inzhener* (engineer) became *inzhenerr*, and *zakon* (law) became *zakonn* (Kuruch 1985: 89, 91, 374, 433). However, some teachers and parents thought that words borrowed from Russian should retain their original spelling in Sámi orthography to avoid confusion; otherwise, it was feared that the special Sámi spellings could spread, leading the children to make mistakes when they wrote Russian.

The Kuruch-Afanasyeva group's alphabet[3] also encountered some criticism. After experimental phonological investigations of the sounds in Sámi words as pronounced by two informants (Eek and Kuruch 1983: 16), the linguists decided to include among other things two letters – *j* and *h* – that do not occur in the standard Russian alphabet, in order to reflect sounds found in the Kildin Sámi language but not in Russian (Alekseyeva 1989: 3).[4] The number of letters in the Kuruch-Afanasyeva group's alphabet was now forty-three – eleven more than the Russian Cyrillic alphabet. Critics claimed that the alphabet had become too complex for young learners, but Kuruch argued that it was necessary to have an 'objective representation' of the language. At a meeting of the Association of the Kola Sámi (AKS), she explained that, 'as a scholar, I can describe what is in the language only from an objective, truly objective, position; and show how to transfer that description to the curriculum, first of all to the semiotic system, and give it all to the school'. At the same meeting, Afanasyeva explained that the alphabet and orthography were in fact well suited for learners since it followed the principle 'what I hear, I write'.

Even so, many teachers soon refused to use both the alphabet and the 1985 Kuruch dictionary in their classes (Kuznetsova 1991: 2). They complained that the special letters were more of a difficulty than an advantage; in particular the letters *j* and *h* caused a stir as they were perceived by some critics to be 'Latin' and hence alien elements in the writing system. At one point, Kuruch complied and offered to change *j* to й – a Russian й with a comma fastened to it – and *h* to ꞌ (apostrophe). Although such modified Cyrillic letters are used in many non-Slavic languages in the former Soviet Union, these too were met with scepticism – particularly the new apostrophe character as some Sámi did not acknowledge the existence of the sound it represented. One of the Sámi teachers who tried to instruct the children in using it felt that it posed a problem for both pupils and teachers. This teacher explained that the Kuruch-Afanasyeva group's special letters could be useful for linguists, but were too confusing for other people (a point shared by some linguists, such as Eek 1984: 239). She further argued that, since the learners as well as many of the teachers were largely unfamiliar with any Sámi language, they needed a more simple orthography:

> We have a young generation of teachers here who are not very confident with the language yet. And the difficulties that have arisen have slowed down the development of the language, the progress in teaching and the publication of textbooks. That's what really happened here.

Kuruch argued that the approach of the Kuruch-Afanasyeva group was correct, not only because it reflected the language objectively and was based on scholarly research, but also because these letters were necessary to reflect Sámi grammar accurately; the sounds had to be represented correctly because they are intrinsically tied to the grammar of the language (Eek and Kuruch 1983: 16). 'One cannot fail to realize and understand that an incorrect representation of phonemes in the letters distorts the structural basis of the words, and that in turn results in the full disorientation of the scholar, the teacher and the pupil as regards the grammatical material' (Kuruch, Afanas'yeva and Vinogradova 1995: 182).

The Kuruch-Afanasyeva group published a book to help teachers understand the rules underlying Kildin Sámi orthography and punctuation (Kuruch, Afanas'yeva and Vinogradova 1995). However, representatives of the Lovozero group protested that the instructors would not be able to understand it: 'With that book even the Sámi teachers need special courses ... the book lies there unused'. The conflict between the Kuruch-Afanasyeva group and those who believed that the proposed alphabet was of greater harm than benefit came to a head when the matter was referred to the provincial authorities. Ten Sámi from the Lovozero group wrote an open letter to the Governor of Murmansk Province, requesting permission to return to the alphabet of 1979.

One of the signatories to this letter stated in an interview that a provincial official informed her that the Sámi would have to agree among themselves on this issue before action could be taken. The bitter character of this conflict is particularly noticeable in that the interviewee quoted below did not consider it necessary or even possible to reach consensus with the opposing faction:

– ... they told us that 'you need to debate this through internally'. I told him: 'We already did.' ... We wrote you a letter that 10 people had signed, 10 people agreed on this....

– *Who are 'you' who agreed on this?*

– That is us, the Sámi, the Sámi agreed among themselves. ... The intelligentsia, those who work with the language ... but he said again: 'you must reach an agreement.' 'With whom?' And he says: 'With Afanasyeva'. Oh! I said: 'We've already debated for 20 years. We'll be debating it for 120 years, we won't reach an agreement. They'll never agree to write it without the 'h' and the 'j' ... [and] the teacher's won't write it like that...'.

Afanasyeva spoke out against the very same letter to the authorities at a meeting of the Association of the Kola Sámi. She argued that, firstly, the provincial authorities lacked the authority to reach any decision regarding the alphabet and, secondly, the authors had offered no real arguments in this letter for why they wanted to revert to the old alphabet.

Meanwhile, Antonova and Kert had already published dictionaries using the older 1979 alphabet, a move that Kuruch criticized:

Both books bring to the school incorrect representations of the structure of the Sámi language, creating in the children a false association of sounds and letters, precluding a correct scientific description and explanation of the morphological variations in the language's system, and thereby consciously vulgarizing the Sámi language and creating unending difficulties in its study. (Kuruch, Afanas'yeva and Vinogradova 1995: 182)

Kuruch further accused the Orthographic Commission of the Ministry of Education of 'incompetence, inconsistency and prejudice' for allowing such books in the schools (Kuruch, Afanas'yeva and Vinogradova 1995: 181). Afanasyeva similarly criticized the Ministry of Education for its handling of Sámi linguistics (Podol'skaya 1992: 2).

It is not for us to judge which actors in this complex linguistic conflict were in the right. However, it is clear that the proliferation of contradictory alphabets, orthographic systems and dictionaries was disadvantageous for such a small language (see, e.g., Klaus 1987: 149). Many Sámi came to the conclusion that the conflict ultimately damaged the language and lessened the prospects of its revival. One teacher, a person who seemed not to belong to either faction, complained:

When they fought, they would come to us at the school. [Someone from the Lovozero group] would come when we were working by the Kuruch system and tell us: 'you don't know anything, the children don't know anything.' Then [someone from the Kuruch-Afanasyeva group] would turn up, and we would be working according to Antonova's system. Again they would criticize us. All the children failed in the dictations, with tears in their eyes.

The Latin Versus the Cyrillic Alphabet

In the midst of the debate as to how Russian Sámi should be written came an alternative suggestion: returning to the Latin alphabet which, it was argued, would bring Kildin Sámi closer to the other Sámi languages and might narrow the cultural and communicational divide between the groups (Beach 1994: 159). Another main argument was that using the Latin alphabet would avoid the problems related to the conflict over Cyrillic alphabets and orthographies.

However, the core group opposed the proposed transition to the Latin alphabet. Kuruch herself stated in a speech to the Association of the Kola Sámi (AKS):

> Steps towards the Latin script were taken in 1993 and weakened, weakened the Sámi language. And because of this the Sámi people suffered, the teachers suffered, the children suffered … there is already a scientifically based and accepted alphabet, and in order to change it a sufficiently high level of support would be needed.

At the same meeting, Afanasyeva put forward a systematic set of arguments against a transition to the Latin alphabet. Firstly, she asserted that the Kuruch–Afanasyeva group's alphabet is not too difficult for the children as they learn the Russian alphabet in the first grade of school anyway and the special Sámi letters only in the second grade; secondly, it is easier for the adults to read something based on the Cyrillic alphabet with which they are already familiar; thirdly, it would be too difficult to retrain the instructors to teach the Latin alphabet; finally, more than fifty textbooks had already been written in the Cyrillic alphabet and would have to be transliterated or discarded if the Latin alphabet were to be used.

Despite these good and numerous arguments against the Latin alphabet, the critics were not entirely convinced. Regarding the most general point underlying Afanasyeva's arguments, that in most ways and for most of the Russian Sámi it is easier to deal with the Cyrillic alphabet – many disagreed. Some Lovozero teachers emphasized that, in any case, the children would ultimately have to learn the Latin alphabet for German and English classes, and for parts of the older generation who had been taught using Chernya-kov's 1933 alphabet, the Latin alphabet has always been the 'correct' one.

Although currently no major debate exists over Latin versus Cyrillic letters, support for Latin orthography is still to be found, such as from the then (2010) leader of the Russian Sámi youth organization, *Sam' Nurash,* Anna Afanasyeva:[5]

> It would be very useful to make Latin orthography for Kildin Sámi. That would be a considerable help in uniting the Russian Sámi with the others. The existing Cyrillic orthography is a barrier, the majority see it as 'more Russian than Sámi' as no one can read this language except 500 Sámi in Russia. Perhaps that [using the Latin alphabet] could help to attract the interest of other Sámi people to the Sámi language of Kola and give encouragement to Sámi in the territory of Russia.

Perceptions of Motivations

The impressive number of works produced by the language revival's core group in a short time bears witness to its collective effort since the mid-1970s and its great 'drive' towards the goal of revitalizing Kildin Sámi. Despite the obvious zeal and personal sacrifice made by these linguistic pioneers, interviews conducted in the 1990s revealed that quite a few of the Russian Sámi had come to perceive some activists as mainly interested in the material gains and other benefits that ensued from studying them and their traditional language. Some informants used words like 'self-interest' or 'profit' when explaining how they understood the activities of certain linguists. The following quote from a Lovozero man may serve as a typical expression in this discourse, which rather mercilessly condemns both groups in the conflict: 'they argue, they write in the newspapers, they're on the radio, and this is their "bread" ... But nobody reads their ABCs and nobody will read them ... they [the ABCs] are not useful for anybody else'. The existence of such attitudes posed a great practical problem for the core group as those who expressed such views were also part of their 'constituency' – the people who were supposed to benefit from their work.

Those Sámi interviewees whose negative attitudes were mainly aimed at the Kuruch-Afanasyeva group often stressed a perceived lack of contact with the general Sámi populace and Sámi language teaching in particular. As it was precisely the Sámi and the revival of the Sámi language that the group was working for (see, e.g., Kuruch, Afanas'yeva and Vinogradova 1995: 4), these informants felt that if the group lacked contact with the 'grassroots', it should face its limitations. Not surprisingly, many of those who criticized the Kuruch-Afanasyeva group from this position expressed more trust in members of the Lovozero group, indicating that they had closer contact with 'the people', those who were supposed to use the language. Such attitudes reinforced the resistance towards using the linguistic work of the Kuruch-Afanasyeva group, which was already being criticized for perceived pedagogical weaknesses.

Yet the Lovozero group also had problems relating to a lack of trust in some of its members, due to the role some of the teachers had during the Soviet era. As a Sámi woman from Lovozero explained:

> Just ten years ago people started speaking Sámi. ... Before that, it was completely forbidden. Even the teachers, the Sámi teachers [tried to] stop them from speaking Sámi. ... But now the teachers themselves go around asking the old people how Sámi words are pronounced.

One Russian Sámi studying in a Nordic country discussed an activist in the Lovozero Group:

> [The reindeer herders] who are between 30 and 40 [years old] don't like her because they remember when they were forbidden to speak Sámi, their mother tongue. And she herself forbade them to speak it, saying that one should learn Russian, learn to speak it well, and that it was essential to study it.

Another Sámi man, who had been relocated from one of the 'liquidated' villages to Lovozero, also recounted the role of this particular activist as a former opponent of the Sámi language in education and life and one who convinced him that his mother tongue was not worth anything:

> And when I came to Lovozero ... in the sixth grade ... she told me: 'learn to speak in Russian, and then speak in Sámi'. ... I told her, I didn't know Russian very well, because I had learnt Sámi from the beginning. Mother spoke to me in Sámi, father in Sámi, everything in Sámi everywhere. We spoke in Sámi at home, we weren't allowed to speak in Russian ... if I spoke in Russian [my father would] say: 'what, are you a *rus*, or what? Stop that at once'. ... And then [she] says 'no, you don't have the right to speak in Sámi. You should speak Russian better than Sámi'. She was right. I learnt to speak in Russian, and I even don't teach my son Sámi. I already feel, like her, why speak in Sámi?

It is important to bear in mind that much of what happened during the Soviet period was not up to the individual; this is also true of the teachers discussed here. Similarly, it is important to note that this kind of attitude on the part of teachers was not unique to the Soviet Union. Indeed, teachers in Western Sámi-speaking areas also told their pupils, and their pupils' parents, much the same: do not use that language, it has no value (see Minde 2005: 18–27). Sámi everywhere had been indoctrinated to believe that their culture and language were worthless when compared to the majority cultures, so it should come as no surprise that teachers of

Sámi origin were not immune to the massive ideological pressure of Russianization, Norwegianization, etc. From Norway, we know that many people who repudiated their Sáminess never went back to it, even when the political climate changed; to this day, many people of Sámi heritage condemn Sáminess as irrelevant or worthless. Against this background, praise is perhaps due to the former agents of Russianization who actually decided to change course.

The important point is thus not what the teachers felt it necessary, appropriate or good to do at that time, but rather the fact that the impression many Sámi got of their teachers during the Soviet period lingered on, even after they began working for the rebirth of the language. Their new course led some Sámi to see the teachers as lacking in integrity rather than as honest activists, which naturally weakened trust in their projects and methods.

Finally, it is important to be aware that such attitudes towards the first linguistic activists are far from universal. Many Russian Sámi hold people from both the Kuruch-Afanasyeva group and the Lovozero group in high regard, perceiving them as having done their best to improve the situation of the Sámi.

Language of the Land, Language of Books

Another obstacle to the learning of Sámi was the differences between the language spoken at school and that spoken at home. Some men from families in which Sámi was still spoken complained about the difference between 'their' language and the language spoken by the teachers, which they felt was not suited for those who actually knew some Kildin Sámi already:

> If I speak to [the teacher] in my Sámi language, she won't understand me, she won't get it, she'll say 'he doesn't know' and that's all, 'get out!' And to anyone who says a couple of such incomprehensible words, she says 'I'll teach you, you'll learn to speak Sámi from me'. But how does she teach, who has she taught? She hasn't taught anybody. ... Nobody has learned to talk, nobody. ... Why don't the children know, why doesn't my son know the Sámi language? Because he can't understand the teacher.

> The children come back from the tundra speaking Sámi too, and then they have to go to school. But they don't want to study Sámi because it's not *the same* Sámi. They say 'I don't understand what they are saying there, they teach me to talk differently'.

This is not uncommon among the Northern Peoples. For example, Vakhtin (1997: 172–176) gives a technical linguistic analysis of the phenomenon in Yupik, demonstrating and quantifying the 'artificiality' of sentence structure and vocabulary in current Russianized usage. Such incongruities between spoken and formal language may make it difficult to establish a synergy between school and the family, in turn making language revitalization more difficult.

Some people thought that the 'unnaturalness' of the school language was rooted in a lack of communication between the academics responsible for systemizing and teaching the language on the one hand and the people who spoke it on a daily basis – often rural people without higher education. Hence, the differences between school language and home language reflected a class divide of sorts, related to the split between the urban and the rural 'poles'.

It is an almost universal phenomenon that 'book language' differs from the 'language of the land'. Nor is it uncommon for sharp conflicts to arise over how best to revitalize a language that has long been subject to repression. Take, for example, Norway's internal language dispute in the 1800s over whether to 'Norwegianize' the Danish writing system in use at the time – an idea especially popular among urban intellectuals – or to create a new written language based on dialects spoken in outlying areas of the country. The conflicts that arose back then make the internal disputes among the Russian Sámi intelligentsia pale in comparison and resulted in a situation in which even today there are two parallel, official Norwegian written languages. The difference lies in the fact that the Kildin Sámi situation at the time of the Soviet collapse was far more critical than that of the Norwegian language in the 1800s.

It is important to note – and learn from – how internal divisions within the intelligentsia and inadequate communication and trust among would-be learners, teachers and linguist activists created severe stumbling blocks in the initial attempts to revive Kildin Sámi. These factors caused additional challenges to the rebirth of the language at a point when the situation was already critical. On the other hand, these are quite common problems associated with language revitalization efforts; there is nothing unique about the events and mechanisms discussed herein. However, because of the extraordinarily weak position of Kildin Sámi, these problems became far greater obstacles to success than they would have been for a language that had more speakers.

We cannot say whether or not Kildin Sámi will be spoken on the Kola Peninsula a few generations from now. It might be that another Sámi language will be in active use in any case – namely, North Sámi. In the following chapter we look into some possible linguistic consequences of educational cooperation between the Russian and Nordic Sámi, which began in the 1990s and is bound to have a long-lasting impact on ethnopolitics on the Kola Peninsula. Tomorrow's Russian Sámi leaders may well have completed their higher studies at institutions closer to home than Herzen University, although still located across a state border.

Notes

1. For a concise overview of the development of Soviet language policy, see Vakhtin (1997: 164).
2. In our transcription system soft sign is transcribed as ' and hard sign as " when referring to quoted or referenced authors – so that readers can seek out the original Russian literature (cf. the overview of the transcription system at the beginning of the book). But when just mentioning invidvidual actors in passing in the text, we do *not* transcribe the soft and hard signs, in order to ensure readability. Consequently, the surname Afanasyeva, which contains a soft sign in Russian, is spelt without an apostrophe when we are referring to her as a political actor, and with an apostrophe when she is listed as an author. Since this is the only such inconsistency that arises, we have chosen to keep this system.
3. A first version of the alphabet was put forward in 1979, and was used in Antonova's ABC (1982) and Kert's 1986 dictionary (Eek and Kuruch 1983). In 1982, the core group announced a modified version of this alphabet (Kuruch, Afanas'yeva and Vinogradova 1995: 181).
4. The letter *j*, also written as **й**, denoted the sound *yh* or dry *j* (Kuruch, Afanas'yeva and Vinogradova 1995: 180). The letter *h*, also written as an apostrophe, was defined as 'preaspiration' – 'an h-like fricative before which the preceding vowel is pronounced with a higher pitch and a stronger intensity than a vowel not followed by preaspiration' (Eek and Kuruch 1983: 22).
5. Interviewed in autumn 2009.

CHAPTER 5

EDUCATIONAL REORIENTATION

Sámi Education in the Nordic Countries

Ethnic Revival, Education and Culture

Education is one of the main mechanisms for reproducing culture and is therefore often identified as a key tool of ethno-politics. Indeed, Anthony D. Smith describes in a primordialist perspective how nationalist intellectuals see education:

> [Education is] a process by which the individual comes to realise his role in the particular historic culture in which he has been brought up, and simultaneously to understand the history and destiny of the community to which his fate is linked, by birth and residence or choice. There is no 'education' outside the community; and no 'community', properly understood, without the self-consciousness that education instils. (A. Smith 1981: 127)

In a more instrumentalist vein, Thomas Hylland Eriksen writes:

> Education can be an efficient aid in the establishment of standardised reifications of culture, which are essential in the legitimation of ethnic identities. Mass-produced accounts of 'our people' or 'our culture' are important tools in the fashioning of an ethnic identity with a presumed cultural continuity in time. (T.H. Eriksen 1993a: 91)

Thus, regardless of whether culture is understood mainly as something essential and ancient or as a symbolic function of ethnic identity, education is important to its propagation. This fact has inevitably come to bear upon the ethnic revivals of the Northern Peoples, whose ethno-politics often press towards changing the way in which their children are schooled, as pointed out by Vitebsky (1990a: 352; 1989a: 217), among others. Education is one of the aspects of the Russian Sámi ethnic revival in which the Nordic Sámi have been very much involved.

Since the early 1990s, people on both the Nordic and the Russian sides of the border have striven to give Russian Sámi youth the opportunity to attend Nordic Sámi educational institutions. Some early key players in this process were the University of Tromsø, the Sámi University College in Guovdageaidnu and the now-closed Sámi Folk High School[1] in Kárášjohka, all located in Norway. Thus, in this chapter, we begin by discussing the roles of Nordic Sámi educational institutions relative to the role of the formerly dominant university institutions for Russian Sámi, using the Nordic institutions in Kárášjohka and Guovdageaidnu as examples. The second part of the chapter presents a case study of an exchange programme between two Sámi educational institutions, focusing on certain negative consequences of this particular instance of cross-border cooperation. This latter part of the chapter is in essence a study of a particular case of cooperation gone wrong, and we urge the readers not to form their main impressions of Sámi cross-border educational cooperation solely based on the events described there. Many such cooperative ventures have taken place, and many of them have been significantly more successful. However, we still feel that it is valuable to shed light on some less fortunate episodes as well.

From South to West – Replacing the Educational Centre

Kárášjohka and Guovdageaidnu municipalities are situated in the innermost part of Finnmárku, Norway's northernmost county, and are Sámi cultural strongholds – not least because the language has been preserved there to a larger extent than in most other places in the Nordic countries. Both municipalities have their share of the Sámi institutions that have been founded in recent decades, including various educational and research establishments.

The ties between Lovozero District and Kárášjohka Municipality had already been forged by the time the Soviet Union collapsed, as the two were twinned in 1990 (Kuimova 1990: 2; Nystad 1999: 5). According to Lars Johnsen (interviewed in 2009), former principal (1991–99) of the Sámi Folk High School, his institution had its first experience with Russian Sámi students when the Kárášjohka-Lovozero Friendship Association rented rooms at the school for two Russian Sámi who were participating in an exchange at the local secondary school. In a 2010 interview, one of these students, Pyotr Popov, told us that they had come to Kárášjohka after a series of academic tests in Russia, in which thirty or so students had participated but only two were selected in the end. Since the Folk High School had few pupils at the time, these two Russian Sámi also became part-time students at that institution in 1992. Some years later, the Folk High School began to work with the Friendship Association to give more young Sámi people from Lovozero the chance to study at their institution. Some of the Russian Sámi involved in these exchanges stayed to take additional business management- and media-related subjects at the Folk High School.

Several of the academically successful exchange students went on to study at the Sámi University College in Guovdageaidnu, the University of Tromsø or elsewhere in the Nordic countries. As for the Sámi University College, its former principal (1989–96) Jan Henry Keskitalo informed us that contact between the college, Herzen University and the Murmansk State Pedagogical Institute (since 2002, the Murmansk State Humanities University: see MSPU 2011) had started in the mid-1990s. The Guovdageaidnu–Herzen cooperation began when the University of Tromsø's Centre for Sámi Studies, Tromsø Museum and the Norwegian Ministry of Municipal Affairs' office for Sámi issues contacted the Sámi University College about the possibilities for creating an indigenous academic cooperation involving Russian actors. A framework agreement was signed between the Sámi University College and Herzen University in the mid-1990s, and the first group of students came to Guovdageaidnu in the autumn of 1996. This arrangement was open to students from any of the Northern Peoples, not only Sámi.[2]

Nordic Sámi education rapidly became a coveted opportunity in Russian Sápmi. Consequently, it developed into a major form of contact between the Nordic and Russian Sámi and a great opportunity for the Nordic Sámi to contribute to the strengthening of the Sámi identity among the Russian Sámi. Indeed, pan-Sámi ideology was one of the reasons that the Nordic side became interested in border-transcending education cooperations, as former principal Lars Johnsen explained:[3]

> It was part of our philosophy that this was to be a school for all of Sápmi. Hence, we were not only preoccupied with Lujávri [Lovozero], but also active in the South Sámi area. Also, we had courses in the Coastal Sámi area, in Oslo and in Trondheim....[4]

The importance of Nordic Sámi education for the Russian Sámi is especially discernible in the fact that it began to replace the prestigious Herzen University in St. Petersburg as the most sought-after place for higher education.

One of the more progressive aspects of the Soviet nationalities policy was that ethnic minorities, including the Sámi, were accorded special quotas for admittance to Herzen University and other institutions of higher education. The number of places set aside for groups such as the Sámi varied. For example, in 1989, three places were set aside for the Sámi at

Herzen, one at Petrozavodsk University, one in Arkhangelsk and three at the Pedagogical Institute in Murmansk. As early as 1931 a special Sámi section had been set up at the Murmansk Technical Secondary School (Kiselev and Kiseleva 1979c: 2). The quotas were mostly filled by Sámi students from the Lovozero area, but they were also open to Komi and Nenets (Rogozina 1989: 4). For Sámi youth, Herzen University, along with the Pedagogical Institute in Murmansk and Petrozavodsk University in Karelia, became the gateway to a career and the key to good salaries and heightened social status. However, since perestroika, Nordic Sámi institutions have provided Kola Sámi youth with opportunities to travel and live in the West, learn foreign languages and obtain knowledge, know-how and networks that effectively prepare them for active roles in the Russian Sámi – or even pan-Sámi – academic and political leadership.

At the same time as educationalopportunities appeared in Nordic Sápmi, studying at Herzen increasingly became contingent upon the financial resources of the individual student. One former student explained: 'With a five-year study programme and all, one has to consider one's strengths and options. Nowadays in these unstable times [the late 1990s] one needs finances, and therefore it is especially difficult right now. Before, when I went there, things were still stable.'

During the 1990s, economic instability and hyperinflation in Russia turned previously ample government grants into small change, while dilapidation and poor social conditions in the state-run student hostels made them less attractive. At the same time, the high cost of non-student housing in St. Petersburg meant that such an option was an unthinkable alternative for most students. Going to Herzen had become far more difficult in practical terms for most Sámi youth.

The combination of the simultaneous decline of Herzen and rise of Nordic Sámi education created great opportunities for pan-Sámi nation-building by drawing the people of the Russian Sámi areas closer to their Nordic kin. This brought many Russian Sámi to the Nordic countries, giving them the opportunity to acquaint themselves with the North Sámi language and culture, introduce them to Nordic Sámi politics and society and influence their identity and worldview (Corbett 1996: 53). At the same time, it created an arena in which the Nordic Sámi could learn about their eastern kin and create a deeper understanding among Sámi from both sides of the former Iron Curtain about differences and similarities within their border-transcending nation. Finally, the replacement of educational centres outside Sápmi with Sámi ones ensured that the young intelligentsia of the Russian Sámi did not lose their Sámi identity. Quite the opposite, Nordic Sámi education served to reward and encourage self-identification as Sámi.

The Selection of Students

In selecting Russian students to go to Nordic Sápmi, a combination of the hosting institutions' desires and processes in Russia played a role. According to former principal Jan Henry Keskitalo of the Sámi University College, their institution wanted students who were Sámi, or had some competence in a Sámi language, or wanted to study either Sámi language or traditional Sámi handicrafts. However, Herzen ultimately decided who would go to Guovdageaidnu.[5]

As for the Sámi Folk High School, former principal Lars Johnsen said that they wanted students who were young Sámi with good academic capabilities and good general behaviour, who would ultimately return to Lovozero and become local resources. They also sought to achieve a fair gender balance. The National [Sámi] Culture Centre in Lovozero assisted in the recruitment, and representatives of the Folk High School informed the local community about the exchange during school trips to the village.[6] In addition, they sent one of their first two Russian Sámi students – Pyotr Popov, who had by now become a teacher at the Folk High School following further education at Guovdageaidnu – back to Lovozero to publicize the exchange opportunity. Popov told us that he used, among other things, adverts in the local newspaper and word of mouth to attract new groups of interested students, doing his best to search out 'those who were [academically] good, those who I thought could learn the language'. The final decision was made by the headmaster, after deliberation with Popov, in his capacity as a teacher with special responsibilities, and with the Friendship Association.[7]

Although it is quite understandable that selection processes focused on those with the best potential to do well academically, some of our informants felt that one group that perhaps ought to have be given access to education in Nordic Sápmi missed out: people of more rural origins, from families without any tradition of higher education, who were also the ones who had a better grasp of Kildin Sámi. As one of the Russian Sámi who studied in Nordic Sápmi in the 1990s explained:

> In Lovozero practically none of the youth know [Sámi]. … I have in mind those who go to school, who complete, say, middle schooling … I'm not talking about the young reindeer-herding kids, whom they would of course never send [to the Nordic Sámi institutions].

Among many in Lovozero who hoped to send their children to Nordic Sápmi for education, the general impression was that knowing Kildin Sámi would be of little advantage, but that strong academic skills were necessary – in particular, knowledge of foreign languages. Although it would make little sense to send someone who was academically weak to a foreign school, where it would be necessary to learn a new language in addition to mastering the curriculum, it is unfortunate that this seems to have constituted a barrier to representatives of the rural, land-oriented end of the class and cultural continuum.

Kildin Sámi Versus North Sámi?

It could be argued that pressure to perform well in other school languages took time, resources and energy away from the learning of Kildin Sámi. Back in the late 1990s, when some of the people who could speak a bit of Kildin Sámi were asked why they were not making greater efforts to pass it on to their children, one of the reasons they gave was that the children already had enough work with English and German at school and that those languages would be more important if they wanted to go to Nordic Sápmi anyway. This also mirrors a certain perception of Nordic Sámi education as not just a form of education particularly relevant for their ethnic group, but also as a gateway to the West. For some students, going to Nordic Sápmi and learning the North Sámi language was not only a goal in itself, but also a stepping-stone for learning other languages, such as English or Norwegian.

Another reason for stressing foreign language skills was that the children had to learn the North Sámi language from scratch once they crossed the border. Knowledge of other foreign languages and practice in dealing with them were seen as definite assets in order to handle the Nordic Sámi curriculum. A few Kildin Sámi-speakers perceived North Sámi as directly competing with Kildin Sámi, as two young informants put it: 'Very many young people see that North Sámi can give a lot more in the future than Kildin Sámi can, and many want to study precisely North Sámi …'.

The attractiveness of North Sámi over Kildin Sámi stems in part from its possible usage when it comes to communicating with ethnic kin in a wider area; one of our informants, a Russian Sámi student in Norway, aptly referred to it as 'the international Sámi language' [*mezhdunarodnyy saamskiy yazyk*].[8] This is indeed the position that North Sámi has in today's international Sámi society. Although some seemed to view this as a North Sámi cultural imperialism of sorts, it could also be argued that it is more valid to see it as the displacement of vernaculars by a national language and culture (see Anderson 1983/1991: 45) – a process often associated with nation-building (Gellner 1992: 244). However, an important caveat to this latter view is that the difference in status between North Sámi and Kildin Sámi is not that of a vernacular and a 'national language' – instead, the two are simply distinct languages, where one is stronger than the other. In any case, the perceived competition caused some Russian Sámi to be less enthusiastic about the popularity of North Sámi, as this interviewee explained:

> Since we live in Russia, we should first of all know our own Kildin dialect. ... But in Lovozero, everybody thinks that the other's better: 'What do we need the Kildin dialect for?' In Lovozero I have often heard things like that. 'What's the point of the Kildin Sámi dialect when everybody is going to Karasjok [Kárášjohka] and studying North Sámi?' ... The Scandinavian Sámi are harming the Sámi, the Sámi of Murmansk Province, and the Kildin dialect is vanishing. They subtly draw our children to study the North Sámi dialect rather than the Kildin one.

The statement of 'subtly drawing children away' to study North Sámi instead of Kildin Sámi is of course rather conspiratorial, in view of what seems to have been the intention on the Nordic side. According to Lars Johnsen,[9] serious consideration was in fact given to using Kildin instead of North Sámi, but it was decided that this would not be practical:

> That was the big difficulty, choosing ... North Sámi or Kildin Sámi. The discussion went on for quite a while. But the situation was that Kildin Sámi was in the minority. What we wanted was to raise the status of the Sámi in Lujávri [Lovozero], and there's much status in having studied abroad ... and getting into a foreign school ... also, they would learn something new and become local resources. Another issue was how in the world were we to teach them Kildin Sámi when they were already having difficulties doing that in Lujávri? It was not easy finding people who knew that language.

Johnsen relates that his institution did try to arrange a brief course (sixty-four hours) in Kildin Sámi in Kárášjohka, but unfortunately no participants applied. However, in the 1998–1999 school year, the institute successfully arranged a multiple-week Kildin Sámi course in Lovozero, which was attended by the Russian Sámi students studying at the Folk High School. In 1999, the institute even actively considered building up a department of their school in Lovozero, with 'local language competence', but the practical, legal and financial challenges were considerable.

The dire situation of Kildin Sámi caused some Russian Sámi to feel that the choice might be between North Sámi and no Sámi language at all. As former student Pyotr Popov was to say, ten years after his exchange experience: '...it would of course be better if it's one of the local languages. ... But it's better that it's one of the Sámi languages rather than none of the Sámi languages. Those who carry the [Kildin] language are mostly older people and, well, they are dying, leaving us...'.

Resource Infusion or Brain Drain?

The time spent studying in the Nordic countries has given many Russian students a stronger Sámi identity. One student who had never known Kildin Sámi, but learned North Sámi on the other side of the border, went from thinking of himself as Russian to thinking of himself as Sámi:

> I think that the Western Sámi help a lot, among other things, by waking us up to the fact that we are Sámi. For example, I didn't know Sámi when I came to Norway, and I basically thought of myself as Russian [*russkiy*], like the rest of the Russians [*russkiye*]. But now that I've learned North Sámi I also want to learn Kildin Sámi. I already feel Sámi inside.

This possible mechanism should also be noted in the debate over North Sámi and Kildin Sámi: learning the one might provide an impetus to learn the other and would also make it easier to grasp Kildin Sámi. The two languages are quite different, but there are enough similarities that knowing one would be a definite advantage in learning the other.

Returning to the matter of Sámi identity development, the former student Pyotr Popov said that, although he had always considered himself a Sámi, this identity had been reinforced by his experiences across the border:

> Learning North Sámi became a window in my world. … One had to go to Norway to see that Sámi was valuable, not until then did I begin thinking about my own identity. In Russia, I did know I was a Sámi. But that's just one of several hundred peoples in Russia, while in Norway I saw that there was the Sámi Parliament and the Sámi Radio and that the language was being used.… [10]

The effects described by these informants reflect some of the stated intentions of Nordic Sámi institutions that became involved in the student exchanges – namely, facilitating a revitalization of Sámi identity and the status of Sáminess locally. Yet educating cadres abroad always entails a risk: those individuals who were supposed to return with renewed enthusiasm and competence may opt to remain in the 'receiving' country.

Arguably, internalizing pan-Sámi ideology may make it more likely that Sámi students do not return to their home countries; after all, in the extreme consequence of this worldview, Sápmi is the home country, not the various nation states that have carved borders through it. Hence, a Sámi may emigrate and yet to some extent still be 'at home'. Other factors may also cause a brain drain: when leaving for study abroad, a student may sincerely intend to return, but not make it back for other reasons, such as finding a partner who does not want to leave his or her homeland. Others again find themselves unwilling to return after having studied abroad for a while, having grown accustomed to the culture and lifestyle of the receiving country. A Russian Sámi girl who chose to stay in Russia for her studies said:

> Of course we owe a big thanks to Norway, to Karasjok, Kautokeino [Kárášjohka, Guovdageaidnu] and all those people who have engaged themselves in this. The kids like studying there a lot, but when I spoke with one of them, she said she couldn't imagine what she would do in Lovozero, even though she does have teacher training.

Another Russian Sámi said about the students that she wished 'that they would be of some use to their people back home ... but very often they just want to stay there'. There are, however, quite a few exceptions. Many of the Russian Sámi students have returned to Russia, and there are certainly those who would not wish to spend the rest of their lives in Nordic Sápmi. As student and *Sam' nurash* activist Sergey Gavrilov[11] said:

> In Scandinavia, the economic conditions are very good, but to stay here and live here [pauses]. ... In the Nordic countries the lifestyle is punctual and regular and slow. Young people aren't always satisfied with this. Because of this, a lot of guys return to Russia. Although there are many girls who stay here.

The risk of brain drain is not something that has suddenly arisen with the advent of Nordic Sámi education. Most students who went away to study in the cities during the Soviet period stayed there too (Mikhnyak 1993: 2). A Russian Sámi student completing her degree at Herzen in the 1990s said that many of those who studied there did not wish to return to their home villages in the North: 'Clearly many finish their studies and want to stay in the city, they don't want to go back to Lovozero, and not just to Lovozero but also other villages in the North. ... And I'm like caught between the two: I like it here and I'm pulled there.' She went on to explain how it would be difficult to return to Lovozero:

> In Lovozero you can realize yourself, but in what sense? One the one hand I could practise my profession. That is to say, I could go there and work as a teacher, implement new methodology .... But on the other hand I know, and people have already told me, that 'you won't realize yourself there. You wouldn't be able to work, because the old generation wouldn't let you break out, let you show what you know – even though what you know is interesting enough'.

This, of course, is not a problem unique to the Russian Sámi or to indigenous peoples as such. All over, people from rural areas who go on to higher education in urban areas often do not find it possible or even desirable to return to their place of origin. It may also be that the difficulties of returning to the Kola Peninsula villages were actually more substantial for those Sámi who spent five years as young adults in Russia's second largest city (St. Petersburg) than for those who undertook their education in another small Sámi village, but across the border. Even so, it remains a fact that the Nordic Sámi educational institutions inherited Herzen's risk factor – the potential for pulling Russian Sámi youth away from Russian Sápmi.

The Big Differences

The risk factors listed here – brain drain and possible competition between the North and Kildin Sámi languages – led a few informants to feel that Herzen and Nordic Sápmi served the same function: replacing Russian Sámi culture with the culture of a more powerful external society. However, several differences exist between the impact of Herzen and Nordic Sápmi as educational centres.

The education at Herzen University, while producing research on Sámi matters and eventually contributing to the formation of a Sámi civil society elite, also contributed to cultural Russianization. The Herzen experience in many cases replaced Sámi identity and culture with Russian or Soviet identity and culture; when students returned home, they sometimes even tried to impose this on the children of those who had stayed at home. In contrast, the Nordic Sámi institutions actively cultivate Sámi identity and encourage people to work for the preservation and development of their culture. Indeed, the explicit purpose of these institutions is to strengthen Sámi culture. If the Nordic Sámi institutions have contributed to a brain drain and introduced a threat to Kildin Sámi in the form of North Sámi, this has run counter to their own intention, which has been to 'educate them [the Russian Sámi] and send them back to become local resources'. Furthermore, the Nordic Sámi institutions in fact want the Kildin Sámi language to survive, which has resulted in several revitalization efforts with funding and expertise (technological, pedagogical) from Nordic Sápmi.

We should also not underestimate the symbolic effect of these institutions being explicitly Sámi rather than representing the dominant majority culture. For the intelligentsia educated in Nordic Sápmi, Sáminess will not be seen as a thing of the past or relegated to the periphery, something worthless and futureless. Instead, they will identify Sáminess with the modern and resource-endowed institutions where they received their education.

A Case of Cooperation Gone Wrong

The Two Institutions

In this section of the book, we describe how one specific Sámi exchange programme developed, focusing on its negative outcomes. We have chosen to do this in order to demonstrate the potential risks associated with cooperative ventures between partners in countries with great economic differences, such as the Nordic states and Russia, particularly during the 1990s. We have sought to do our very best to anonymize the actors involved as our point is not to show *which* institutions were involved, but rather *how* the cooperation played out. Therefore, we simply refer to them as 'the Nordic institution' and 'the Russian institution'. We are aware that identifying these institutions will not be difficult, but we have chosen to account for the events described below despite this as we consider it important to demonstrate how things can go wrong as well. As for those readers who cannot restrain their curiosity and will therefore attempt to determine the institutions to which we are referring, we would remind them that this case is now more than ten years old. It would be highly unfair to form any judgements about these institutions today based on what happened back then.

The cooperation involved a Sámi educational institution in one of the Nordic countries and a Sámi educational institution in Russia. A document published by the Nordic institution about the cooperation opened with the following lines:

> The preservation and development of the culture and traditional livelihoods of indigenous peoples receives priority in [our internal] as well as in [our] international projects. The work of [the Nordic institution] has always been directed towards the preservation and development of traditional Sámi customs and related livelihoods. In Russia, in Murmansk Province, [the Russian institution] works with the same aims. ... An agreement between the two schools has been signed, mainly aimed at joint work in the teaching of reindeer herding and Sámi handicrafts.

As the document indicates, the main aspect of the relationship between the institutions was the preservation and development of Sámi culture. Accordingly, this was a case of explicit cooperation between the Russian and Nordic Sámi with the official aim of furthering Sámi culture (also see Sashenkova 1998c: 5).

Cooperation is Initiated

Teachers from the Nordic institution made their first visit to Murmansk in the late 1980s and were told of the Russian institution by a member of the Russian Sámi intelligentsia there. It took another year before the teachers made direct contact with their Russian counterparts to exchange knowledge about Sámi handicrafts. In 1990, the headmaster of the Nordic institution and a few students visited the Russian institution and examined the possibilities for official cooperation, for which the international political climate was beginning to seem ready. In 1991, an official agreement was signed. The first part of the agreement concerned the training of Russian Sámi teachers and subsequent teaching of Sámi handicrafts at the Russian institution. Discussions were held about closer collaboration in the teaching of reindeer herding, and the first steps were taken towards the creation of a common reindeer-herder programme, which took several years to get going.

In 1994, the Russian institution was granted the right to a 'productive base' under the provincial special programme for the development of reindeer herding in its district, which in turn came under the Federal Programme for Economic and Social Development of Small Northern Peoples until the year 2000 (Kuznetsova 1997a: 2). Thus, in order to give reindeer-herding students real-life practice, the school would have its own reindeer herd and corrals. It was also an indication from the Russian authorities that they were open to collaboration with the Nordic institution. In December 1994, the provincial administration transferred 177 million roubles for the creation of this productive base (Kuznetsova 1997a: 2).

The Russian Institution Expands

In 1996, the Russian side set up a reindeer-herding branch in another small village, a former Sámi settlement. The village in which the Russian institution was situated is henceforth referred to as 'Russian village 1', while the locality of the new branch is referred to as 'Russian village 2'. The headmaster, an ethnic 'Russian', later stated that 'if the school hadn't come here, then it would have been the end for these people' (Andreassen 1997: 2). Most certainly, Russian village 2 was feeling the crisis of the late 1990s: industrial sites were closed, the old *sovkhoz* had collapsed, and unemployment was very high. The idea was that the Russian institution would take over the old *sovkhoz* and use it as the base for the Nordic–Russian reindeer-herding course. The students at the two institutions would study under the same programme, spend parts of their courses visiting each other and learn each other's languages. The project would be funded by the two governments, with the Ministries of Education and Foreign Affairs in the Nordic state in question covering the larger part.

In sum, this was a well-funded and promising project. It had the official blessing of the Barents Secretariat[12] and the governments of both states, and could draw on substantial resources in both countries (Andreassen 1997: 2). In addition, the course was attractive to prospective students, with opportunities to learn foreign languages, travel abroad and perhaps also continue their studies at universities in the receiving country. It promised to give reindeer herding a new start and new prestige among the Russian Sámi.

Under this project, the Russian institution would develop modern reindeer herding according to the model applied in the Nordic state. In addition, it was hoped that the project would bring employment to Russian village 2 in the form of a reindeer-herding renaissance. At that time, it had been more than twenty years since the Soviet authorities had eradicated the last traces of reindeer herding in that area. It was hoped that the return of the reindeer would revive the almost extinct local Sámi culture and identity in the district. According to staff at the Nordic institution at the time:

> ...there are about a hundred Sámi [in Russian village 2] ... But they don't speak Sámi, for example. They've forgotten it. Nor do they know Sámi handicrafts, only the grannies knew them, and many of them are dead now. Now nobody knows. In the autumn we had a visit from two women from the Sámi Association [of Russian village 2], the head and the vice-head. They studied handicrafts here for two months. They had never done any handicrafts before.

Role Reversal: Who Benefits?

In 1996, the two sections of the Russian institution swapped roles: the school's official address was moved to Russian village 2 along with the higher administrative staff, while Russian village 1 was to host just a subsidiary section. Many of the school's most valuable assets were transferred to Russian village 2 (Kuznetsova 1997a: 2; 1997b: 5). In addition to the removal of equipment, money for publications was stopped, five staff members were fired and seven vacancies were closed (Kuznetsova 1997a: 2). Not surprisingly, this caused friction between the administration and the staff still working in Russian village 1. One member of the local Sámi intelligentsia described how the 'Russian' headmaster:

> suddenly decided to move [to Russian village 2]. And here they didn't even inform the staff. And when they had moved almost everything there, he told the staff that basically the school would be over there, and here there would be like a branch. For all of last year it operated like a branch. He really offended them, took away everything, literally everything, including the sewing machines, took away everything, all the machinery, and didn't leave a thing. So how were they going to avoid antagonism? And then he started paying them badly, holding back their salaries.

The headmaster was accused of mismanagement and corruption in several papers in Murmansk Province (Kuznetsova 1997a: 2; 1997b: 5; Vdovina 1997: 4, 5). During 1995 and 1996, salaries and stipends, already undercut by inflation, were with few exceptions held back. Meanwhile, accusations against the headmaster and his closest co-workers of increasing their income and expenditures manifold gradually came to feature in the local media; a scandal ensued, and the conflict sharpened. The headmaster went to court against one of the newspapers and the journalist who wrote the article that first made the scandal public (Kuznetsova 1997a: 2). Relations between the headmaster and staff who remained in Russian village 1 gradually worsened, until the staff there challenged their headmaster publicly, and a bitter legal battle ensued over both the rights to the name of the institution and the material property of the school. During a meeting at which the staff from Russian village 1 requested dissolution from the section of the school at Russian village 2, the headmaster reportedly told them: 'I reject all your accusations. I have been audited by many – there are breaches, but nothing criminal. Don't rush your decision ... you'll fall on your face. After all it is we who have a programme with financing [with the Nordic institution]. Here all is empty' (Kuznetsova 1997b: 5).

Despite the headmaster's confidence, the staff in Russian village 1 won the struggle, and towards the end of 1997 the two branches of the school were formally separated, with the section in Russian village 1 retaining the name of the institution (Kuznetsova 1997d: 1; Sashenkova 1997: 6). In addition, the provincial educational administration decreed that the inventory taken from Russian village 1 to Russian village 2 should be replaced. The newly elected headmaster of the Russian institution personally travelled to Russian village 2 and reappropriated the photocopier, among other things.

After the separation of the two branches, the Nordic institution declined to work with the re-established Russian institution in Russian village 1 and remained focused on the international reindeer-herding project at Russian village 2. Teachers from the Russian institution complained that the cooperation:

> isn't continuing, because the headmaster who was [here] before, moved the school to a different village ... and those contacts, those connections went with him [to Russian village 2]. All the worse for us. [Now instead] we would like to develop our relations with ... some kind of Sámi educational institution in [another Nordic country].

In practice, the Russian institution had most of its ties with the Nordic institution severed and went in search of other Sámi partners in the Nordic countries (Sashenkova 1998b; 1998c). Meanwhile, the Nordic–Russian reindeer-herding project collapsed from within. Most significantly, the very basis of the herder training – the herd itself – gradually disappeared. According to staff at the Nordic institution, the former headmaster bought 100 reindeer in addition to the 900 he transferred from one of the two large reindeer-herding companies on the peninsula, making an initial herd of 1,000. By late 1997, there were some 200 reindeer left – not much to base a revival of reindeer herding on, much less a revival of Sámi culture.

Perspectives at the Nordic Institution

In 1998, the headmaster of what had now become a separate educational institution in Russian village 2 was removed by the provincial authorities for misconduct. Until this point, there had been minimal contact between the re-established Russian institution and the Nordic institution, and the latter knew little or nothing about the conflict with the headmaster. Having recently and belatedly learned about the headmaster's dismissal, staff at the Nordic institution had the following to say at the time:

> He left of his own will. We think that he's always been very good, effective, hard-working. Our cooperation was always good, we always got good results. Sometimes we argued, but as brothers. We were of differing opinions, but always discussed things openly, even very difficult questions. We always trusted each other.

Upon being told that lately much had been written in the Russian newspapers giving the impression that the headmaster had exploited the relationship between the Russian and Nordic institutions for his own purposes, one of the people at the Nordic institution asked in reply:

> – How was it advantageous to him? What interest did he have in us?
>
> – *But that's what the newspapers say. … Well, cars, flats and things like that….*
>
> – It's not true.
>
> – *It isn't true? So all those newspapers are mistaken?*
>
> – It was already like that when we started up in 1991, then too there was always somebody criticizing him for going abroad, asking who had the right to do that.

The Nordic partners seemed to feel that the reason for the scandal was narrow-mindedness towards people with entrepreneurial skills and initiative. Certainly, it was difficult to be an enterprising leader in post-Soviet Russia. The former headmaster was far from alone in experiencing resistance and prejudice when trying to carry out projects that could have benefitted all parties.

In addition, a tendency exists among some Nordic actors to feel that outsiders should not meddle in or even comment on Russian Sámi politics because they are the internal affairs of the Russian Sámi. As a teacher from the Nordic institution explained:

> It has to be said that what goes on in Russia is their own business. It's a different state, and they solve their own problems there. We wouldn't like it either if they were to come here and deal with our issues. … It's their own internal affair, which we neither can nor wish to solve.

Another attitude worth noting was communicated by one person at the Nordic institution: that the headmaster, being 'Russian', held a competence that the Russian Sámi could not match:

– The main question is not whether it is Sámi who are involved; rather, it is whether we together can produce results that are of use to the Sámi. It is unimportant to us if it is Russians or Sámi who are involved – or [people from our country] for that matter – just as long as it is useful, as long as it makes things better for the Sámi....

– Honestly, if there weren't such a person on the Russian side like the former headmaster, none of this would have been possible. And I honestly don't know a single Sámi in Russia who could have managed what he did. Honestly. Of course, I know that what I'm saying is incorrect, that there must be such Sámi, but until now nobody's ever shown me one.

Clearly, this latter representative of the Nordic institution felt that the Russian Sámi were somehow unable to produce results for their own benefit, that they needed not only Nordic aid, but also to be led by individuals from the majority ethnos of their country. The notion that 'Russians' are needed to lead the Russian Sámi is otherwise unheard of among the Nordic Sámi; rather, the dominant discourse is that the Russian Sámi need Nordic Sámi assistance to help them resist the pressure from Russian society and authorities (Berg-Nordlie 2011a: 26–30, 32–33).

What Went Wrong?

Troubles like those described thus far were not uncommon in Nordic–Russian collaborative ventures in the 1990s. As such, this 'failed case' does not describe a specifically Sámi phenomenon, but rather illustrates the potential dangers of Western–Russian cooperation in general. At the core of the problem seems to be the Nordic side's uncritical trust in one individual leader and the absence of a broader interface with the institution which could have enabled them to understand what was going on. Most probably a main reason for this can be found in the view that one has no business intervening in 'internal politics' on the other side of the state border. The Nordic institution simply did not see it as their business to question decisions made by their contact at the Russian institution.

On the Russian side, some people identified the lack of reaction from the Nordic institution as a kind of donor naïveté. A journalist who wrote on the issue had the following to say about the role of the Nordic side:

But how would they know at [the Nordic institution] about the headmaster's style of leadership? They really don't know, they think they are handing out money to a good cause. ... They might grant the money with the best of intentions: 'Go ahead!

Develop! Resurrect reindeer herding! Start fenced herding! Whatever is possible. Let the young people meet each other! Live well!' But then the headmaster controls the money. ... Yes, obviously they are [naïve] but why? How are they naïve? If they have an agreement, if they want to help, honestly want to help, well if that is naïve then let it be naïve, but it's naïveté of the best kind.

In all fairness it should also be noted that the headmaster would not necessarily have seemed untrustworthy at the outset. In fact, he was generally seen as a man who had done much good for the Russian institution – also among the local Sámi:

I realized that obviously he's a dishonest person, mercenary. And so his hands are dirty. That's what I came to think. But the fact that he's crafty and business-minded, of course I haven't forgotten those qualities either. ... To be honest, when he came, [the Russian institution] hardly existed. It existed, but at such a low level that it was simply embarrassing. He raised it and deserves a big plus for that, and it should never be forgotten.

This interviewee added that, although he might have been 'avaricious', the headmaster did realize that the Russian Sámi and Russian village 1 were the foundations of what he was doing. However, the involvement with the Nordic institution changed all that as the economic basis was now on the other side of the border, and the headmaster's activities became oriented towards cooperation with a foreign institution. A somewhat uncomfortable conclusion may be that, had there been no cooperation project, the headmaster would not have had the opportunity or the incentive to act in ways that caused serious internal conflict within the Russian institution, and eventually led to his removal from the position of Headmaster.

That said, this project also produced some positive outcomes. The Sámi of Russian village 2, for example, have mixed feelings about what happened:

– They did get the *sovkhoz* going, and we kind of latched onto reindeer herding; when you think about the fact that the *sovkhoz* in [our village] was almost bankrupt and we hadn't even thought about setting up a school, it seemed maybe the reindeer herding would save us somehow. So we grabbed the chance ... we only found out through the newspapers how the headmaster brought the school to us....

– People started seeing, they acquired an interest in feeling Sámi. Because the school that is in [the Nordic country] is also kind of a Sámi school, and the basic ties, although not those between the headmasters, are all the same, specifically at the level of Sámi culture. It raised the level of awareness even among people who are only to the slightest degree Sámi. I know that there are even people who are in their late thirties and who've re-registered themselves as Sámi.

Although in many ways this affair did some harm to the Russian institution, and not much good when it came to reviving Sámi culture in Russian village 2, it did a lot in terms of revitalizing the local Sámi *identity*; thus, at the very least even this 'failed case' could be described as a partial success. Moreover, contacts between the re-established Russian institution and the Nordic institution were eventually resumed after the headmaster in Russian village 2 was dismissed by the provincial authorities. By then, his energy and innovation in setting up the cooperative project with the Nordic institution had inspired his former employees at the Russian institution to link up with a similar institution in a second Nordic country.

Notes

1. 'People's high schools' (Norwegian: *Folkehøyskole*, North Sámi: Álbmotallaskuvla) are a type of pre-university college, often specializing in various kinds of creative education.
2. Jan Henry Keskitalo, interviewed in autumn 2009.
3. Lars Johnsen, interviewed in autumn 2009.
4. The South Sámi area consists of the middle and lower northern parts of Norway and Sweden; the Coast Sámi area basically consists of the coast of Finnmárku and Romsa/Troms counties in Norway.
5. Jan Henry Keskitalo, interviewed in autumn 2009.
6. Lars Johnsen, interviewed in autumn 2009.
7. Pyotr Popov, interviewed in autumn 2009.
8. Sergey Gavrilov, interviewed in autumn 2009.
9. Lars Johnsen, interviewed in autumn 2009.
10. Pyotr Popov, interviewed in autumn 2009.
11. *Sam' Nurash* is an organization for young Russian Sámi. This quote from Gavrilov is from spring 2010.
12. The Barents Euro-Arctic Region was established by Norway, Sweden, Finland and Russia in 1993, with the aim of strengthening financial, political and social integration in the Barents Sea littoral, including the indigenous peoples of the area.

CHAPTER 6

POLITICAL REPRESENTATION

The Intelligentsia

The term 'intelligentsia' refers to people with higher education and is in essence synonymous with 'academics' or 'intellectuals'. It is also used self-referentially by those to whom it applies, often invoking a special role and duty in society – or, as one of the Russian Sámi members of this group of people put it: '[The intelligentsia are] those who bleed with their whole heart for their people, for its problems; and who try to raise the people, to support [it]'. As Nistad (2004: 12–13), referring to the intelligentsia of Imperial Russia, wrote:

> In sociological terms, the intelligentsia could be defined as a separate group in society, consisting of thinking people who feel that they by the power of their knowledge and education have a duty to function as the moral voice of the people and release their fellow creatures from barbary and suppression … [it] was a moral category, and it consisted of people who felt they had to liberate the people through fighting ignorance and suppression.

In some ways, this description also fits the intelligentsia which emerged from the Soviet system, in which individuals engaged in widespread self-identification as intellectuals with a particular responsibility for the rest of society. The intelligentsia of the Russian 'Northern Peoples' were no exception. In a 2002 anthology about the Russian indigenous movement, one article focuses on this group of people, defined broadly by the author (Haruchi 2002) as 'people working in culture and arts, technical fields and science and practicing in the Arctic, such as teachers, doctors, artists and others'. According to Haruchi, the post-Soviet indigenous movement in her region (Yamalo-Nenets Autonomous Area) began when, in the 1980s, the local intelligentsia started questioning their own role in society: did they actually identify with their own people and represent them, or were they supporting state policy and betraying their own? When political events caused a window of opportunity to open, the intelligentsia started looking for ways to preserve their people's ways of life and to work for their welfare; after some time, they became an important positive force, a group of people 'aware of its responsibilities and historic role at a given stage in history' (Haruchi 2002: 92). What Haruchi is talking about here is a process that occurred in many places in the Soviet Union at the same time. The collapse of the state led to a shift from a top-down ethnic organization to a situation in which independent projects of ethnic revival were possible. The intelligentsia of many ethnic groups vigorously seized the opportunity to help their peoples build a new future. In Gramscian terms, they attempted to move away from being 'tradition intellectuals' and become 'organic intellectuals' (Gramsci 2001: 1138).

Another factor that pulled the intelligentsia towards ethno-politics was that the economic crisis resulted in fewer, less stable and less economically attractive openings for people with university degrees; attaining leadership in a civil society organization was thus also a potential means of employment. Although such insight is important, we should take care not to fall into 'the instrumentalist trap', where we see only material interest in everything politicians and activists do. It would have been easier for the ethno-political activists simply to pursue normal, 'Russian' lives and not engage in activities that at times were – and are – considered to be sufficiently radical by the regional authorities to merit unwanted attention. Undeniably, ethno-political leadership can have its benefits, but it is also often a life spent fighting – and perhaps never winning.

Even so, ethno-political leadership involves definite benefits and, as we shall see, quite a few of the Russian Sámi at the grassroots level came to read some of their leaders' activities as motivated primarily by self-interest. For many critical observers, such distrust in leader figures also rubbed off on the organizations headed by these leaders, thereby seriously weakening ethno-political cohesion and hampering the development of early post-Soviet Sámi political life. In fact, distrust in certain leader figures who were active during the 1990s was still evident on the Kola Peninsula in 2011.

In this chapter, we present the roots of the distrust, which means that we will again have to focus on some less-than-fortunate episodes in Russian Sámi politics. The reader should bear in mind that the Russian Sámi movement has also done some very good things for its people – things to which we return in the conclusion. But this chapter does not focus on those things; rather, it seeks to explain why many people came to feel that the early leaders and organizational structures of the Russian Sámi did not represent them properly.

AKS: The First Post-Soviet Russian Sámi Organization

Founding of the Association of Kola Sámi

Work towards the creation of a non-governmental organization to embrace all the Sámi in Russia started in February 1989 (Podol'skaya 1992: 2; Orgkomitet 1989: 3), and the AKS was founded on 3 September the same year (Alekseyeva 1989: 3; Rantala 1994b: 203; Lobanov 1991: 1). The constituent conference took place at the Murmansk Institute for Advanced Teacher Training (Alekseyeva 1989: 3). According to our informants, the new organization was the concept and initiative of the Head of the Institute, the linguist Rimma Dmitriyevna Kuruch.

The founding conference of the AKS was called at short notice because it was feared that the authorities might attempt to obstruct it. Indeed, the provincial authorities did send two representatives, who made great efforts but failed to talk the Sámi out of founding their own organization (Rantala 1994a: 316; Kolpakova 1991: 2). The conference was chaired by Vasiliy Selivanov, then employed at the geophysical laboratory in Lovozero and associated with the Kola Science Centre (Alekseyeva 1989: 3). Seventy people attended the meeting, and Selivanov was elected as first president of the AKS (Podol'skaya 1992: 2), with Kuruch and Nina Eliseyevna Afanasyeva as vice-presidents (Orgkomitet 1989: 3; Kolpakova 1991: 2). Selivanov had previously served as the government-sanctioned representative of the Russian Sámi to the Nordic Sámi Conference in Ohcejohka/ Utsjoki in 1983 and had also met a group of Finnish Skolt Sámi who came to Lovozero on a brief visit earlier in 1989 (Rantala 1994a: 316; Selivanov 1984: 1). The election of Selivanov thus represented a degree of continuity with Russian Sámi affairs prior to perestroika.

Voronov (1989: 1), who was the editor of *Lovozerskaya pravda* at the time, wrote in *Northern News* two months after the founding of the AKS:

> The Association of Kola Sámi is an independent public organization which is called upon to promote social and economic development of this ethnic minority, to preserve its traditions based on the harmony of man and nature, and to study and develop its cultural and spiritual heritage.

According to the first article of its constitution, the AKS is 'the plenipotentiary of the united ethno-dialectical groups of Soviet Sámi on the Kola Peninsula in the USSR and abroad, and has as its aim to protect their rights and interests' (Orgkomitet 1989: 3). In other words, the organization effectively set out to be not only a group of activists fighting for the Sámi people, but also the representative organ of *all* Kola Sámi.

Less than a year after his election as first president of the AKS, Selivanov was granted a post in the Lovozero administration, and the Executive
Committee of the AKS decided that his new job was incompatible with
holding the presidency. Afanasyeva was elected president in the summer
of 1990 and remained the leader figure of that organization for the rest
of the period covered here – in fact, she only stepped down relatively recently, in 2010. Around the time Afanasyeva became AKS leader, Kuruch
left the AKS on the grounds that she was non-Sámi and that only Sámi
could be full members.

The AKS held its first proper annual assembly in 1991 (Lobanov 1991:
1), with 107 participants in attendance, in addition to numerous observers from the Nordic countries and from Estonia (Kolpakova 1991: 2).
Afanasyeva was re-elected, with her son as the only opponent, and he subsequently became vice-president (Rantala 1994a: 317; Kolpakova 1991:
2). This led some of the Russian Sámi to start discussing whether or not
the organization was functioning in a sufficiently democratic way.

Highly Contested Elections

The events described in this section of the book were by their very nature
controversial and caused a deep split among the politically active Sámi
in Russia, which in turn had a negative impact on a young organization
that needed to establish its legitimacy. Different versions of these events
abound, but our account is based on elements that most of those involved
agree on.

The problems started when the time came for AKS to hold its next
presidential elections. The first of what developed into three rounds of
voting took place in the early autumn of 1995 and was held in Murmansk
in the hall of the *Oblast Duma* (provincial parliament), with approximately
one hundred participants, including some Nordic Sámi observers. Three
people ran for the presidency: Nina Afanasyeva, Zinaida Kalte and Anna
Prakhova. According to some informants, the original list of presidential
candidates had included only two – Afanasyeva and Kalte – but there
were protests from the floor that Prakhova was supposed to be on the list
as well and after some discussion she was included. In the first round of
voting, no candidate secured the necessary number of votes, and it was decided that there was to be a second round of voting between the two top
candidates: Afanasyeva and Prakhova. However, the meeting was quickly
dissolved, and the second round was not held until several months later,
in December 1995 (Antonova 1997: 2). Again, accounts differ as to what
actually happened during this round of voting – and also about the events
leading up to it – but most say that Prakhova won. However, Afanasyeva

and her faction claimed that Prakhova's victory was not in line with the rules specified in the statutes of the organization; thus, they called for a new ballot on 21 December 1996 (Antonova 1997: 2). This third round of voting was held in the industrial city of Monchegorsk. At that time, only one person stood as candidate for the presidency: Afanasyeva. Antonova of the Lovozero group commented scathingly on this election in an article in *Lovozerskaya pravda*, calling it a 'joke' (Antonova 1997: 2). Many seemed to agree with her, but others again supported Afanasyeva's position that the second round had not been held in correspondence with the rules.

Regardless of what really happened in this rather confusing set of events, there can be no doubt that it was unfortunate for the post-Soviet Russian Sámi movement to suffer such a deep political split at this early stage in its history. Although political competition and conflict is intrinsic to any community, the devastating thing in this case was that the conflict had played out in a way that led many people to lose faith in the very system – that is, the internal democracy of the AKS.

The Organizational Landscape Expands

The Revival Fund and the Aid Society

The Kola Sámi Revival Fund (*Fond vozrozhdeniye kolskikh saamov*) and the Sámi Aid Society (*Obshchestvo pomoshchi saamam*) were two other early examples of Sámi civil society activity. The Kola Sámi Revival Fund was founded in 1991 by Kuruch, after her departure from the AKS (Lobanov 1991: 1). Great ambitions were proclaimed for the Fund, its aims including better education and job creation for the Sámi and the re-creation of historical Sámi settlements that had been 'liquidated' during *ukrupneniye* (Lobanov 1991: 1). However, the Revival Fund's application for registration as a charity was rejected, and it was instead registered as a TOO – a public limited company (V. Bogdanov 1997: 6). The Fund thus became a purely private business under Russian law, but retained its name and ties to the Sámi cause. A few years later, the Sámi Aid Society was founded jointly by AKS President Afanasyeva and Kuruch (V. Bogdanov 1997: 6).

Rumours of improper conduct in these organizations soon began to spread in the Russian Sámi community. One example of this was the 'sausage affair', involving a large consignment of reindeer sausage donated from a source in Northern Norway. In 1997, news appeared in the Murmansk papers about a Norwegian brand of reindeer sausage being sold illegally in Murmansk (see, e.g., Kumunzhiyeva 1997: 4). Investigation by the Provincial Trade Inspector and the hygiene authorities revealed that the sausage had passed the expiry date, lacked the appropriate certificate of production and ingredients, and seemed to originate from an individual highly placed in one of these two organizations. Upon confrontation, the individual in question admitted to selling the 37 kg of sausage that the authorities already knew about. It was further revealed that the sausage had been sold without the special permission necessary for the sale of humanitarian aid, which is otherwise against Russian law. The authorities were more concerned about the faulty standard of the sausage than its abuse as humanitarian aid, and fined the person responsible for 'the sale of sausage products not complying with the required standards, without a certificate and guarantee from the producer' and which had passed the expiry date (Kumunzhiyeva 1997: 4). Among the Russian Sámi, however, many were more preoccupied with the fact that aid intended for them had been received by an organization nominally working for their benefit and had then been sold without their knowledge and possibly for personal gain. Stories like these, some verifiable and others only rumours, served to undermine popular trust in the Russian Sámi organizations.

The Revival Fund and the Aid Society also had problems with their requests in the name of the Russian Sámi. While stating their cases in terms of the rights of the Sámi and Sámi culture, neither organization could show any mechanisms to ensure representativeness, such as elections. Nor could they show that they had a set of explicit guidelines or intentions set out in organizational charters or other public documents by which their activities and achievements could be judged, as illustrated by the inability of the Revival Fund to provide such a charter for a freshwater fishing application in 1997. Kuruch said it would enable her to preserve the reindeer herd that the Fund was attempting to establish, create new jobs and preserve Sámi culture (V. Bogdanov 1997: 6). The lack of such documents was criticized at the time, but the Fund still got the permit, despite protests from the Provincial Ichthyological Service (V. Bogdanov 1997: 6).

In short, these organizations never managed to connect with their constituencies and establish transparent mechanisms of representation that would give the Kola Sámi a sense of ownership in them. That, in turn, undermined the ties between the discourse of the two organizations and their actions; the arguments that a reindeer herd owned by one of them constituted a revival of independent Sámi reindeer herding or that fishing quotas for them would mean the revival of lakeside, riverside and coastal Sámi communities were at best difficult to prove, as long as there were no mechanisms for popular representativeness and participation.

Social Background, Gender and Leadership

In addition to perceptions of democratic deficits and corruption within the movement, it was also a problem that a certain kind of people held the reins while others were kept on the sidelines. As we have seen, the original Russian Sámi organizations were propelled by a group of people almost all of whom had university education and whom many other Russian Sámi perceived as somewhat distant and detached from their lives – the intelligentsia.

The case of an urban intelligentsia developing into an ethno-political elite both fits various theories about the role of the intelligentsia in ethnic revivals and matches similar processes among other groups. The two most obvious comparisons are with the other Russian Northern Peoples and the Nordic Sámi. The situation at the founding conference of the Russian Association of Indigenous Peoples of the North (RAIPON)[1] in 1990 sums up the situation of most of the Northern Peoples: 'There were very few fishermen, hunters and reindeer herders among the delegates. A large number were intellectuals and people from the field of culture and the arts. ... Half of the delegates were members of the Communist Party' (IWGIA 1990: 14).

The problem of social background, representation and legitimacy is a classic one with new ethno-political movements. Numerous instances of intelligentsia-driven, urban-based ethnic revivals have occurred among groups such as the Maori (Pearson 1988), the Breton (McDonald 1989) and eighteenth- and nineteenth-century European nationalist movements (Hobsbawm 1990: 104; Argyle 1976). This latest example brings us to another point to bear in mind: not only indigenous movements, but also the ethnic revivals of larger groups have been controlled by urbanized intelligentsia who are often remote from the grassroots of their own people. Thomas Hylland Eriksen has suggested that perhaps 'the leaders of a dominated group must master the cultural codes of the dominant group in order to present their case efficiently' (Eriksen 1993b: 129).

This tendency has been noticeable among the Nordic Sámi as well. For example, a landmark in the development of Norwegian Sámi organizations was the founding of the Sámi Society in 1948 in Oslo, by urbanized diaspora Sámi (Hætta 1994: 158; Stordahl 1991: 26; Otnes 1970: 174–177). Still, an important contrast between the Russian and the Nordic Sámi is that among the Nordic Sámi there have also been powerful organizations spearheaded not by urbanized intelligentsia, but by people engaged in land-based activities, perhaps most notably the Norwegian Sámi Reindeer Herders' Organization (Berg 2000: 137, 212). We should also remember that the iconic main organizer of the first border-transcending Sámi conference (1917) was a reindeer herder – namely, Elsa Laula Renberg, whose political base was in South Sápmi, a region where Sámi identity is rather closely associated with this profession.

Many factors contributed to the initial dominance in Russian Sámi ethno-politics of not just urban intellectuals, but specifically female urban intellectuals. *Ukrupneniye* and the replacement of nomadism as a way of life with 'production nomadism' were particularly effective on the Kola Peninsula, possibly due to the shorter migration routes there, compared to many other parts of the Soviet Union (Kuoljok 1985: 127). Most *siyt*s on the Kola Peninsula would move less than a few hundred kilometres, which might have made it easier to send the men off on their own in controlled brigades while the women and children stayed behind in the villages. The women were to a larger extent than the men cut off from the rural, traditional way of life, acquiring a more urban lifestyle – which for some involved seeking higher education, or even developing academic careers. The result was that the Russian Sámi intelligentsia and subsequently its early ethno-political leadership were essentially a group of urbanized, university-educated women (Yefremov 1993b: 2).

Another explanation, given in a 2009 interview by Ivan Matryokhin (at the time leader of OOSMO, a Russian Sámi organization which we present below) explained female dominance in the early leadership through the following mechanism: (i) it was only natural that the first leaders would be those Sámi who had higher education; (ii) higher education had been accessible for the Sámi mainly at the Herzen Pedagogical University and Murmansk Pedagogical Institute; and (iii) in the Soviet and Russian tradition, pedagogical universities have been dominated by women. We should also note the following statement of *Sam' nurash* activist Tatyana Matryokhina:[2] 'People involved in Russian civil society organizations are quite often women, while men hold official executive positions and other top jobs in society'. In essence, what is being said here is that women hold high positions in organs of less power, whereas men hold high positions at the levels where most decisions are made.

Regardless of the causes, the distance in social background between the political leaders and the other end of the Russian Sámi social continuum – combined with the skewed gender distribution – constituted yet another obstacle to building popular legitimacy and reduced the potential of the new organizations as harbingers of cultural revival and nation-building.

The Leaders and the Nordic Link

If we compare the educational aspects of the ethnic revival (see Chapter 5) with the organizational aspects discussed here, we may say that both forms of activity were to a certain extent externally oriented in that various kinds of assistance were being sought out in the West.

Not only the Sámi in the Nordic countries, but also governments, interstate bodies, and non-Sámi NGOs have provided aid to the Russian Sámi. Getting a full overview of the funds that have flowed from the Nordic countries is difficult, if not impossible. No institution controlled or registered all of the many aid contributions, which took on a multitude of forms. In addition, interest in the Russian Sámi cause has not been restricted to the Nordic countries. Some major sources of funding were to be found in Germany, the United States and Canada, where the Russian Sámi and their culture have a strong appeal as an indigenous cause. The early Russian Sámi leadership had several important contacts in Germany, among them the charity Lappland-Initiative Bremen (Rahe 1997: 1; Rossi 1999: 32), which was set up in 1995 and worked with the AKS (Loginova 1998a: 2; Loginova 1998b: 1).

Many works on ethno-politics see group-strengthening processes mainly as a question of building up the group from within. In contrast, it seems that Russian Sámi ethno-politics initially focused just as much on the outside world – namely, the Nordic Sámi areas and even certain non-Sámi actors. The first Russian Sámi leaders had great success in building up foreign networks and alerting the outside world to their existence and troubles. However, they were less successful when it came to promoting intra-group cohesion.

The Internal Split is Formalized – A New Organization is Formed

Almost a decade after the original Association of Kola Sámi was set up, a new Russian Sámi organization was established in Lovozero, on 11 July 1998. The founding conference took place in the *Dom kultury* ['culture house', youth club] with 109 people present, including delegates from the villages of Afrikanda, Yona, Loparskiy and Tuloma and the cities of Olenegorsk, Monchegorsk and Murmansk (Sashenkova 1998a: 5; Makseyeva 1999: 1).

The new organization was given the name *Obshchestvennaya organizatsiya saamov murmanskoy oblasti* in Russian, abbreviated to OOSMO (Sashenkova 1998a: 5); in English, this translates to 'the Public Organization of the Sámi of Murmansk Province'. Some notable continuities existed between the old and the new organization. First of all, many, if not most, of the people with leadership positions in OOSMO had held similar positions in the AKS, including a former head of the Lovozero section and vice-president of the entire AKS (Avdeyeva, Antonova and Kirillov 1998: 5). When OOSMO made its first official visit to Norwegian Sápmi, this former vice-president was in the delegation (Kuznetsova 1999: 1). In addition, to some extent it was the same university-educated, urban women who took the initiative to create OOSMO. Although the organization's two first leaders (1998–2010) were male (Aleksandr Kobelev and Ivan Matryokhin), the nine other initiators of the organization were women (Sashenkova 1998d: 5). Similarly, five of the six first board members of the weighty Lovozero section of OOSMO were female (OOSMO 1998: 5).

Yet we can also note some important initial differences between the old and the new organization. At the constituent assembly of OOSMO, the delegates expressed 'a lack of faith' in the AKS as the main reason for founding an alternative organization (Sashenkova 1998d: 5). This 'lack of faith' was spelled out in greater detail, including the lack of transparency, concern about financial irregularities, a feeling that AKS had failed to support the Lovozero Sámi in their struggle to protect herding pastures from geological searches for gold and other minerals and – last but in no way least – the fact that the main office of the AKS was located in Murmansk and not in Lovozero (Sashenkova 1998a: 5 and 1998e: 5). Whether the AKS should be based in urban Murmansk or in rural Lovozero, closer to the majority of the Russian Sámi, had been a significant issue already at its founding conference. At the time, it was argued that it was important to be close to the central organs of provincial power (Alekseyeva 1989: 3; see also Orgkomitet 1989: 3). However, as early as the 1991 conference the issue was taken up again (Kolpakova 1991: 2).

Eager to demonstrate its integrity, OOSMO was initially zealous in accounting for its activities. For example, after receiving generous aid from Kárášjohka Municipality, it reported to the public through the pages of *Lovozerskaya pravda* on what had been received and how it had been distributed. These efforts to cultivate transparency and accountability were one factor that increased the popularity of OOSMO from the outset.

An individual who was interviewed in 2009 but preferred to remain anonymous also said that one of the factors leading up to the split had been rivalry over controlling aid from Germany and the Nordic countries, which had begun as a conflict within the first organization. According to this informant, some of the humanitarian donations had been used to the benefit of individuals and their networks and that rivalry over such money flowing in from the West had caused tensions that contributed to the split. As for the AKS president herself, who in 1998 had actively tried to dissuade people from founding a separate organization, she would argue ten years later that the authorities had played a part in what took place, since they had an interest in there being two Sámi organizations rather than one strong and unitary movement and thus did what they could to foster this schism (Berg-Nordlie 2011b: 61–62).

Whatever the reasons for the formation of OOSMO, it is not clear that the existence of two separate Sámi organizations has been as damaging as the initial conflicts within the core group of the Russian Sámi intelligentsia during the 1990s. When asked whether having two organizations was problematic, interviewees often duly reminded us that conflicts between organized groups exist in all societies. One Russian Sámi drew parallels to the conflicts between parties in the Norwegian Sámi Parliament, while a Nordic Sámi compared this situation to disagreements between the early Norwegian Sámi organizations NSR and SLF (cf. Berg-Nordlie and Schou 2011: 7, 12, 25). In terms of participation and representation, it may also in fact be beneficial to have two organizations, centred on different locations, each working to mobilize Sámi people to become active and each providing platforms for their own leader figures.

In addition, there has evidently been room for two Sámi organizations on the Kola Peninsula as both have survived and continue to exist. Today, they have a normalized relationship and collaborate on several matters. The establishment of the Kola Sámi Assembly, for example, was a joint project of the two organizations (Berg-Nordlie 2011b: 65–66).[3]

Thus, we end our account with the decisive move from the AKS-dominated 'unipolar' phase of Russian Sámi ethno-politics to the beginning of the 'multipolar' phase, where a conglomerate of actors operates in an increasingly complex political landscape. The AKS era of the 1990s was an important step on the way from the pre-organizational phase of the late 1970s and the 1980s to the new millennium's multi-organizational situation as it served as a school for political activity, a bridge builder towards the Nordic Sámi and a forum in which to play out internal conflicts. What happened inside, around, and eventually to the AKS during the 1990s set the course for much of what was to come.

Notes

1. The Russian name is *Assosiatsiya Korennykh Malochislennykh Narodov Severa, Sibiri i Dalnego Vostoka Rossiyskoy Federatsiya* (AKMNSS i DV RF). The organization itself uses RAIPON in English-language documents and relations with most non-Russian partners.
2. Matryokhina was interviewed in autumn 2009.
3. This project has in itself been controversial, both due to antagonism between activists and authorities and because of internal conflicts among the Russian Sámi – but in any case, that story falls outside the temporal scope of this book. For more information on the matter, see Berg-Nordlie 2011b.

CHAPTER 7

CONCLUSIONS

In this book, we have focused essentially on a rather small circle of people
and their attempts to build an ethno-political organizational framework
for their indigenous group – the Russian Sámi – and integrate this into
already existing Sámi political structures abroad, and revitalize the culture
of their people. What they undertook was no small task, particularly in
view of the weak position of the Russian Sámi at the outset of the period
studied. Deep gaps existed that needed to be bridged between the Russian and Nordic Sámi as well as between the rural and urban sectors of the
Russian Sámi community.

In the course of the late 1980s and 1990s, the leaders of the Russian
Sámi accomplished a great deal. Ties with the Nordic Sámi were firmly
established despite deep structural differences and cumbersome state borders, Sámi identity was given a powerful boost, and several organizations
were established – two of which lived on to form the backbone of Russian Sámi organizational life. In addition to the organizational and insti-
tutional ties that were formed, numerous cultural exchanges have taken
place; these are outside the immediate focus of this book, but such cultural cross-pollination has nevertheless been – and still is – highly valuable
for the development of the Sámi as a border-transcending people. All in
all, the Russian Sámi have accomplished no small feat and, despite extensive initial troubles, their leaders managed to achieve much in this first
period of their ethno-political movement.

Gender and Representation

A central problem is related to the fact that the impetus for ethno-political
mobilization came from a specific section of Sámi society: a rather small
group of people with higher education who had received their education
far from the Russian Sámi core areas. Although this is not at all uncom-

mon in ethno-political processes, the first post-Soviet Russian Sámi elite also had the distinction of being almost exclusively female.

In recent years, the gender imbalance within the Russian Sámi elite has lessened. The fact that the OOSMO leaders were male until 2010 changed the picture, and several young men have gone on to higher education (often abroad, in Nordic Sápmi) and subsequently taken up central positions in Sámi society. Of the registered *obshchina*s, eleven are headed by men and eight by women; in the *obshchina*-based Council of Representatives of the Indigenous Minorities of the North, six of the Sámi members are male whereas four are female. Conversely, the mainly NGO-based Kola Sámi Assembly (partially in response to which the *obshchina*-based Council was formed) has a gender ratio of six women to three men (CIMN 2011b; KNSS 2010).

Social Background and Popular Legitimacy

The other representation problem related to social background and status is a common one in all societies. People from urban, educated and/or comparatively wealthy strata of society get a head start in life and often see it as natural to acquire an education and training that enhance their competence for participation in politics and administration as well as for leadership. This mechanism gives rise to a representation problem for the political class – the intelligentsia, administration and politicians. The failure to include leader figures from the land-based and rural communities in the early phase of Russian Sámi ethno-politics constituted a fundamental problem for the movement in that it lessened how representative it was and made it more difficult for the leaders to establish connections between the grassroots and themselves.

We have repeatedly noted this missing link between rural people and urban leaders, manifested as scepticism among many in the Russian Sámi constituency towards their leaders. These problems of popular legitimacy were also tied to disillusionment due to what was perceived as excessive infighting over strategies, linguistics and positions – a phenomenon that in itself weakened the movement considerably. Some interviewees were also sceptical towards their presumed leaders due to an impression of improper behaviour, particularly in terms of securing gains associated with Western actors – namely, trips abroad, status and access to aid funding.

However, we should bear in mind that the scepticism against the early Russian Sámi leaders was no greater than that against leaders elsewhere in Russia at the same time. Indeed, during this period, trust in politicians was at an all-time low, and corruption was generally high. Those Sámi interviewed in the 1990s who criticized their own leaders would indeed often compare them to the leaders and bureaucrats in Moscow. As an elderly Sámi reindeer herder said:

> If those Norwegian or Finnish Sámi want to give money, for example, or humanitarian aid, then it would have to go directly [to those who need it]. … [When channelled through the organizations] none of it gets to the small Sámi. It's a natural feeding trough – like Moscow. If it all flowed there, then it would stay there too.

Thus, it is important to remember that these accusations of corruption are not actually a specifically Russian Sámi phenomenon, but are a part of a wider crisis of post-Soviet leadership, a paradigm in which politicians are perceived as focusing exclusively on personal self-enrichment.

Such attitudes were mainly expressed by our interviewees during the 1990s, but a few contemporary interviewees also mentioned that scepticism towards the intentions and activities of leader figures was one reason that the organizations and their organs still encounter some popular suspicion. Others accused the provincial authorities of playing on such scepticism in order to, for example, persuade *obshchina* leaders (who are more often from the non-academic/rural part of Russian Sámi society) not to cooperate with NGOs. Indeed, negative attitudes towards the Russian Sámi NGOs per se have been registered among some of the *obshchina* activists, which has obviously formed at least some of the basis for today's split between the *obshchina*-based council organized by the provincial authorities and the mainly NGO-based Kola Sámi Assembly (Berg-Nordlie 2011b: 64–65).

Challenges in East–West Relations

The Western connection also had certain negative aspects. The willingness of the Nordic Sámi to help their ethnic kin resulted in an influx of aid from institutions and private individuals. The need was indeed considerable in Lovozero, but hardly at the dramatic level that many people in the Nordic countries believed. When aid influx began, it was difficult or impossible for donors to control where it all ended up, and there will always be some people on the receiving side who fall prey to the temptations that such situations create. This aspect of the Nordic aid contribution served to reduce the popular legitimacy of the leadership, since some people unfortunately came to suspect all such leader figures of being oriented towards Western capital rather than towards their own constituencies. In addition, as noted in the previous chapter, one recently interviewed anonymous informant claimed that the presence of foreign aid contributed directly to worsening the internal schisms of the Russian Sámi movement.

Another potential problem is the relationship between the North and Kildin Sámi languages. We previously discussed the notion that North Sámi is threatening Kildin Sámi by making it possible for local youths interested in their Sámi heritage to prioritize this more widely used language, which also gives access to the larger Sámi communities in the West. The death of the Russian Sámi languages would indeed be a cultural tragedy, contributing to the cultural impoverishment of humanity and constituting a defeat in the struggle for Russian Sámi cultural survival. However, it cannot actually be taken for granted that local Sámi youth, deprived of the chance to learn North Sámi, would learn Kildin Sámi instead. It is also possible that the opportunity to learn North Sámi is something that attracts people who might otherwise not study any Sámi language at all.

The Benefits of Nordic Partners

Despite the challenging aspects of Nordic–Russian Sámi relations, the general impact seems to have been positive. First of all, the aid contributions of the 1990s, although they sometimes failed to reach the intended beneficiaries, did make life better for many people during the toughest years. The special access to project aid from the Nordic countries also gave (and still gives) the Russian Sámi opportunities that are less readily available to, for example, the Komi of Murmansk Province. However, the most promising effects of the relationship are to be found not in cash flows, but in the educational and organizational cooperation.

Firstly, the special opportunities for Russian Sámi to receive a Western education are a great advantage when it comes to building up respect for ethnic Sámi in local communities on the Kola Peninsula. If these students return to their communities, they have better chances of becoming successful leaders not only of their own people, but also in their broader multi-ethnic communities. Nordic Sámi education also serves to maintain and strengthen Sámi identity among such potential future leaders.

Secondly, it is clear that the position of Sámi organizations and institutions abroad have inspired and spurred the Russian Sámi leadership on. It has also helped that this inspiration has been followed up with a clear interest from Nordic actors in assisting the Russian Sámi in their efforts to create a local Sámi organizational structure. Perhaps particularly important is the recognition accorded to civil society organizations by the Sámi abroad as these organizations have generally experienced relatively little acceptance from the domestic authorities.

The activity of the early leadership as the de facto foreign ministry of their small ethnic group is among their greatest achievements, making it possible to begin the bridging of the East–West divide that had split

Sápmi for so long. Their reorientation towards the Nordic Sámi has probably changed Russian Sápmi permanently. Prior to the fall of the Soviet Union, the easternmost of the Sámi had become completely estranged from the rest of their people. Even before the Russian Revolution, the Sámi under the Tsar had only limited contact with their kin in the West. Indeed, there were no pan-Sámi political structures of any kind. The Sámi have never been as politically united as they are today, and the Russian Sámi are definitely a part of this unification.

The Legacy of the First Leaders

The early Russian Sámi leadership was active and skilful in cultivating the Russian Sámi cause on a variety of levels: among the Russian Sámi themselves, among the non-Sámi on the Kola Peninsula, among the Nordic Sámi and among other groups abroad. Although they can perhaps be said to have had an excessive focus on foreign actors, while being less successful in establishing in-group cohesion, a positive Sámi identity still became more widespread as a result of their activities. However, the divides between the rural and urban, educated sectors of the Russian Sámi community that they faced were not overcome – and hence still constitute a necessary lens through which one should interpret indigenous politics on the Kola Peninsula.

In the new millennium, the Russian Sámi political landscape has expanded to include such entities as the local community- and kinship-based *obshchina* organizations, *natsionalnye kulturnye avtonomii* (national cultural autonomies), the Provincial Centre for Indigenous Minorities of the North, the Council of Representatives of the Indigenous Minorities of the North, and the Kola Sámi Assembly (cf. Berg-Nordlie 2011b: 61–71). Russian Sámi politics has steadily grown more complex since its beginning, when there was only one circle of pioneering cultural activists centred on Nina Afanasyeva and one dominant non-governmental organization (AKS). Although the new complexity has its drawbacks (such as the lack of an organ which is both officially and popularly acknowledged as representing all the Sámi of Russia), it also enables an increasing number of people – and different sections of the Sámi populace – to become involved in Sámi politics.

The abundance of Sámi political actors we meet in contemporary Russia stands in stark contrast to the picture that emerges when we look back at the political landscape in which the Russian Sámi political and cultural activists of the late 1980s and 1990s had to operate; when they began their attempts to salvage Russian Sámi language and culture, and build up an organizational infrastructure for their people, the Russian theatre of Sámi politics was largely empty. They started with almost nothing, but they left as their legacy – among other things – institutionalized ties to Nordic Sápmi, alphabets and orthographies, two major Sámi organizations and a whole new consciousness about Sáminess. As one of the young Russian Sámi studying in the Nordic countries in the late 1990s remarked:

> Before, nobody knew, we were all dispersed and many lost, lost the ties to the Sámi people. Afanasyeva worked a lot on that, found a lot of people, united them. They started coming to the Association. … It gives the Sámi a place to go, reunites the Sámi.

Indeed, this aspect of the leadership's activities cannot be stressed enough: the revitalization of ethnic identity among the Russian Sámi has undoubtedly been a success. The early Sámi leaders were the main drivers propelling this development. With old controversies gradually fading into the past, many Russian Sámi now give the early leaders much credit for their work. One recent interviewee[1] said of the AKS president in particular:

> She was the first. She was the one who started shedding new light on the Sámi culture, so that people in Russia got to know more about us – like [what they knew about] the other nations. … Of course, I've heard negative things too. You do about all politicians. There are good and bad rumours about all of them, it's a common thing. … It's difficult for me to be the judge about which one of them was the best, but she was the first one.

The evaluation of one individual politician contained in this quotation could perhaps be extended to the early leadership in general; it could stand as a valid comment on the entire group of Russian Sámi ethno-political leaders of the 1980s and 1990s. They were the first to speak up for the Sámi of post-Soviet Russia, and the aggregate result of their activities – although we have cast a critical eye on certain events in this book – includes many positive elements.

Despite the internal conflicts and the problems of achieving broad popular legitimacy, these leaders successfully launched a movement that would subsequently branch out into a complex organizational landscape. They heightened awareness of Sámi identity, made the Russian Sámi a subject in both local politics and abroad, managed to channel funds to the Kola Peninsula aimed to promote the well-being of their group and established a bridge to the Nordic Sámi. A disconnect remains between the rural Russian Sámi – perhaps particularly those involved in land-based professions – and the civil society actors who attempt to represent them. Nonetheless, thanks to what happened in the formative decades of the Russian Sámi political movement, the next generation of Russian Sámi activists did not have to start from scratch. The first generation kick-started a Russian Sámi civil society and did an impressive job involving their long-isolated group in pan-Sámi political and cultural life. They have left behind no small legacy.

Note

1. Pyotr Popov, interviewed in autumn 2009.

Glossary and Abbreviations

AKS:	*Assotsiatsiya kolskikh saamov*, Association of the Kola Sámi.
Artel:	A small group of workers, the main collective unit during the first stage of Soviet collectivization. [Russian]
Duma:	Popularly elected parliament. Exists on the federal, sub-unit and local levels in Russia. [Russian]
FSB:	*Federalnaya Sluzhba Bezopaznosti*, Federal Security Bureau. [Russian]
Guberniya:	Old term for province. [Russian]
Internat:	Boarding school. [Russian]
KGB:	*Komitet gosudarstvennoy bezopasnosti*, Committee for State Security; the institution that preceded the FSB. [Russian]
Kolkhoz:	Collective farm, the collective economic unit that replaced the *artels*. [Russian]
Kulak:	Soviet term for 'rich' farmers, reindeer herders, etc.
Lapp:	Old name for the Sámi people, sometimes still used by outsiders. Considered derogatory by most Sámi and should therefore be avoided.
Lop:	Old Russian term corresponding in meaning – and connotations – to 'Lapp'.
Narodnost:	Soviet term for a smaller ethnic group. This was the 'lowest' form of nationhood in a discourse where *natsionalnost* and *natsiya* were the middle and highest kinds of groups, respectively. [Russian]
NKVD:	*Narodnyy komitet vnutrennykh del*, People's Commissariat for Internal Affairs; institution that preceded the KGB.
Oblast:	Province, a subject of the Russian Federation. [Russian]
Obshchina:	A form of kinship-based non-commercial economic unit for indigenous groups, a product of post-Soviet law. [Russian]
Okrug:	Soviet and Russian federal administrative division. [Russian]
OOSMO:	*Obshchestvennaya organizatsiya saamov murmanskoy oblasti*, Public Organization of the Sámi of Murmansk Province. [Russian]
Pogost:	Refers to a village or *siyt*, an old low-level administrative unit. [Russian]
Rayon:	District or municipality, a lower administrative unit. [Russian]
Rossiyskiy:	Russian by citizenship, as opposed to *russkiy*, which denotes a narrower category of people, usually limited by ancestry or 'blood'. [Russian]

Russkiy:	Ethnically Russian, as opposed to *rossiyskiy*, which simply means 'Russian by citizenship'. [Russian]
Saami:	An alternative, less frequent, way of spelling the ethnonym 'Sámi' in English texts. The 'double a' spelling is correct in Finnish and Russian orthography. 'Sámi' is the way the endonym is spelled in modern North Sámi orthography. As this is the biggest Sámi language, this spelling is preferred by many. In English texts, the term is also frequently rendered without the accent over the 'á', as simply 'Sami'.
Sovkhoz:	State farm, a larger unit in the Soviet collective economy. In the cases to be focused on in this volume, they result from merging several *kolkhoz* reindeer-herding units. The *sovkhoz*es were larger and under more centralized control than the *kolkhoz*es. [Russian]
Siyt:	Group of people who travel between set locations as the seasons change. A part of the old Sámi form of social organization. [Kildin Sámi, corresponds to North Sámi *siida*]
Tallv siyt:	Winter settlement of a *siyt*. [Kildin Sámi]
TOO:	*Tovarishchestvo s ogranichennoy otvetstvennostyu*, Public Limited Company. [Russian]
Ukrupneniye:	Amalgamation or enlargement – the process by which the Russian Sámi and other indigenous groups were forced to leave their villages and move to compact settlements as well as how smaller *kolkhoz*es were merged into *sovkhoz*es. Such 'liquidations of villages without prospects' [*likvidatsiya neperspektivnykh dereven*] took place throughout the Soviet Union. [Russian]
Uyezd:	Administrative division during the imperial period. [Russian]
Volost:	Lower-level administrative unit in Imperial Russia. [Russian]

SÁMI POPULATION ESTIMATES

Table 8.1. Variability in Sámi Population Estimates

This table gives an idea of the enormous variations among estimates of the total Sámi population and its components. A dash (—) indicates that no estimate was made for the part of the population concerned. For more updated estimates, see Chapter 2.

All countries	Russia	Norway	Sweden	Finland	Source
75–100,000	2,500	40–60,000	15–25,000	6,500	J. Henriksen 1998: 34
70–100,000	ca. 2,000	40–60,000	15–20,000	6,500	J. Henriksen 1996: 5
60–100,000	—	30–40,000	ca. 17,000	6,000	Helander 1994: 23
60–100,000	ca. 2,000	40–45,000	17–20,000	5–6,500	J. Eriksson 1997: 78
more than 70,000	—	—	—	6,500	*Geographical* 1998: 52
60–70,000	1,890	—	—	—	Dallmann and Diachkova 1999: 17
65,000	4,000	40,000	17,000	4000	Cranér 1994: 53
—	2–3,000	40–60,000	10–15,000	6000	Nystad 1999: 2
50–100,000	2,000	ca. 40,000	ca. 17,000	ca. 6000	Lasko and Osherenko 1999: 3
60–70,000	—	—	—	—	Lazarev and Patsija 1991: 201
50–70,000	2,000	30–40,000	—	5,700	Sámi instituhtta 1990: 14
60,000	—	—	—	—	Corbett 1996: 52
60,000	2,000	35,000	18,000	5,000	Hætta 1993: 6, 12
60,000	1,500–2,000	40,000	15,000	4,000	Ruong, quoted in Beach 1988: 4
60,000	—	—	—	—	Burger 1987: 11
50–60,000	—	—	17,000	—	Swedish Institute 1991: 1
50–60,000	1,500–2,000	17–20,000	15,000	4,000	Zorgdrager 1984: 11
58,000	—	—	—	—	Burger 1987: 179

Table 8.1. continued

All countries	Russia	Norway	Sweden	Finland	Source
40,000	1,700	—	—	—	Cherkasskiy 1998b: 3
35,000	2,000	20,000	10,000	3,000	Beach 1988: 4
35,000	2,000	20,000	10,000	3,000	Ruong 1975, quoted in Beach 1994: 149
ca. 30,000	1,700	—	—	—	Shumkin 1986: 2
—	—	—	—	ca. 6,000	Pan'shina 1995: 2
—	ca. 2,000	—	—	—	Polyarnaya pravda 1995: 5
—	ca. 3,000	—	—	—	Arvola 1990: 4
—	less than 2,000	40–60,000	15,000	4,000	Beach and Anderson 1992: 220
—	1,700	40,000	15,000	6,000	Rahe 1997: 1
—	slightly under 2,000	ca. 40,000	ca. 20,000	5–7,000	Konstantinov 1997: 14

Table 8.2. Russian Sámi Population Estimates through History

Date	Estimate	Source
Early 1600s	ca. 1,000	Kiselev and Kiseleva 1979a: 21
1716	ca. 1,254	Tanner 1929: 296
1782	1,359	Kiselev and Kiseleva 1979a: 21
1820	ca. 1,000	Tanner 1929: 196
1820s	2,000	Hallström 1911: 266; Tanner 1929: 296
1842	1,844	Castrén 1852: 140
1850	1,695	Kiselev and Kiseleva 1979a: 21
1857–1858	1,605	Kert 1972: 1
1859	2,183	Hallström 1911: 266; Tanner 1929: 296
1861	2,000	Hallström 1911: 266; Tanner 1929: 297
1867	1,995	Hallström 1911: 266; Tanner 1929: 297
1868	ca. 1,200	Tanner 1929: 297
Early 1870s	1,965	Tanner 1929: 297
1876	1,940	Hallström 1911: 266; Tanner 1929: 297
1880	1,749	Hallström 1911: 266; Kiselev and Kiseleva 1979a: 21
1884	1,398	Tanner 1929: 297; Kiselev and Kiseleva 1979a: 21
1886	ca. 2,000	Kharuzin 1890: 83
1889	1,763	Hallström 1911: 266; Tanner 1929: 298
1890	1,750	Hallström 1911: 266; Tanner 1929: 298
1897	1,812	Kiselev and Kiseleva 1979a: 22
1906	1,797	Hallström 1911: 266; Tanner 1929: 298
1926	1,713	Kiselev and Kiseleva 1979a: 23
1926	1,710	Osherenko et al. 1997: 35; Vakhtin 1994: 34[1]
(Murm. Province) 1929	1,730	Kiselev and Kiseleva 1979a: 24

Table 8.2. continued

Date	Estimate	Source
1933	1,806	Kiselev and Kiseleva 1979a: 24
1959	1,792	Osherenko et al. 1997: 35; Vakhtin 1994: 34
1970	1,836	Osherenko et al. 1997: 35; Vakhtin 1994: 34
1971	1,900	Vázsolyi 1971: 855
1979	1,775	Osherenko et al. 1997: 35; Vakhtin 1994: 34
(Murm. Province) 1986	1,705	Belyayeva 1991: 19
1989	1,835	Osherenko et al. 1997: 35; Vakhtin 1994: 34
1989	5,000	Vatonena 1989: 89
1990	1,900	Taksami 1990a: 23
(Kola Pen.) 1992	1,600	Doiban, Pretes and Sekarev 1992: 8
(Murm. Province) 2002	1,769	Rosstat 2002
(Russian Federation) 2002	1,991	Rosstat 2002

Sources: most of the figures and sources here are taken from Utvik (1985: 67).

NUCLEAR BOMB TESTING ON THE KOLA PENINSULA

Little official information is available about the nuclear bomb tests carried out in the Khibiny range, and few of the sources among the Russian Sámi mention them. When asked, people on the Kola Peninsula seem either unaware of the issue or unwilling to broach the topic, even though the tests were mentioned in passing in a small article in *Lovozerskaya pravda* (Kuznetsova 1997c: 3). During his fieldwork in Lovozero in 1991, Beach asked in particular about nuclear contamination, without anyone mentioning the nuclear tests. Only upon his return to Sweden did he learn about them and noted that 'no one I had spoken with in Russia made mention of it, and I doubt they were aware of it' (Beach 1992: 125). During fieldwork for this book in the 1990s, one Russian Sámi did, however, talk about the incident, and the remainder of the quotations in this section are from this individual. The reader should bear in mind that this is the account of only one person, whose narrative remains otherwise unsubstantiated.

The man said he had been working in one of the industrial towns on the other side of the Khibiny range when the bombs were detonated: 'I was there, I saw it all. And I would like to say that there was absolutely no protection. They didn't tell us that it was dangerous, that it was atomic energy, that one shouldn't drink the water. Nobody told us!' Unaware of the tests and their ramifications, the local inhabitants were unable to take precautions against the radioactivity that inevitably followed, especially with the rain.

> And then children started dying in the hospitals, from leukaemia. ... When they began investigating, it turned out that when it rained, and if there was wind from that side ... and if the children had played on the streets without head coverings, then their hair would fall out and they would die.
>
> ...

How could we have known? Nobody knew, nobody, I didn't know and the other guys didn't know. They didn't tell us there'd been a blast, they only said 'experimental purposes, for the Fatherland', that's what they said to us, 'it's necessary'.

The informant claimed that those working for the medical authorities were aware of what was happening to people's health. He went on to say that people were offered double wages and other benefits to go and work at the sites of the nuclear blasts. He knew several people who took up the offer. 'They went … and after two months they were able to afford a car, but then nobody saw them again. They went south and that was it.'

Although no one else spoke about the blasts, this informant said that some people did know about them and also knew that the sites are dangerous: 'The people who know, they don't go there. I know, I don't go there. I don't drink the water there, nor eat the berries, there's nothing there.'

It should be mentioned that the Kola Peninsula also seems to have been affected by the nuclear detonations on Novaya Zemlya in the 1940s and 1950s. In 1990, one local inhabitant wrote to the newspaper saying that he and others remembered the horizon lighting up over the Kola Peninsula when there were nuclear explosions on Novaya Zemlya and that the lichen and reindeer were severely affected by radiation (Filippov 1990: 4).

INTERETHNIC RELATIONS

Sámi and Komi

The first families of Komi migrants to arrive on the Kola Peninsula were Fillippov from the village of Izhma, Terentyev from the village of Bakur, Rochev from the village of Gam, and Terentyev from the village of Neshabozh (Zherebtsov 1982: 195).

It has been held that the Komi migration occurred after a decision by the Tsar from the 1860s permitting the free movement of peasants in Arkhangelsk (to which the Kola Peninsula then belonged) and Vologda *guberniya*s [provinces] (Konakov, Kotov and Rochev 1984: 6). According to Hallström (1911: 283), the first four Komi families that arrived were written into the Lovozero *pogost* before coming there, but later families were denied permission to go to Lovozero. Kiselev (1994b: 3) and Brylyova (1996: 161) give the contrasting and standard version, namely that none of the Komi had prior permission to move to the Kola Peninsula. According to these authors, they first tried to go to the Kanin Peninsula and thereafter the Pomor [Russian coastal settlers] areas in the south of the Kola Peninsula, but were turned back from both places by the locals, and therefore went on to Lovozero (Yefremov, quoted in Brylyova 1990: 2). In order to placate the Lovozero Sámi, the Komi, among other things, paid for the rebuilding of the Lovozero church after it burnt down around 1896 (Kiselev 1994b: 3).

Anti-Sámi Racism

During the Soviet period, there was often a tendency towards an ethnic hierarchy which placed the Sámi at the bottom, the Komi in the middle and 'Russians' at the top. Discrimination and prejudice against the Sámi took various forms. Although reindeer herding and herders were often the main victims, it also reached other levels of the village communities, including the children at the *internat* [boarding school]. A Sámi woman living in one of the closed military zones described how her teachers would matter-of-factly voice the expectation that Sámi pupils would be academically weaker than Russian ones:

– In our class there were such episodes, such unpleasant episodes … there were some boys, Russians [russkiye], who did not understand anything, didn't learn very well, and they [the teachers] started yelling at them: 'you're even Russians [russkiye]! Look at the others', like 'the Sámi who are sitting there, they understand this better than you!' He felt that we should be slower, should be stupid…

…

…… if you're educated, that means you're not a Lapp, but if you're uneducated, then even Russians [russkiye] are called Lapps. A person who's rolling drunkenly around, they'll call him a Lapp. It became an insult to be used against all kinds of low people.

– Why?

– Because they came here, and they felt like that they had a superior culture. We had different clothes and such; for them it seemed uncivilized. There came so many specialists, from the cities.

– These were Russians [russkiye]?

– Yes. They started doing things their way … and now, I tell you … Sámi, non-Sámi, Izhemets, Komi or Nenets, or Ukrainian, they'll call you a Lapp anyway. If you look like a bad person.

The Impact of Indigenousness

With the opening up of the former Soviet Union, the new discourse on indigenousness and the involvement with the Nordic Sámi, the tables have been turned to some extent, although prejudice against the Sámi definitely still exists.

A Lovozero Komi spoke of the greater attention that the Sámi have been receiving since the opening up of the Soviet Union (from Westerners in general and from researchers in particular), the perceived inattention to the Komi and their lack of indigenous status.

– Earlier you said that it would be good if the Komi were to be considered a people of the Kola Peninsula.

– Well, yes, why not? Of course, it's nice when there's interest.

– And many people have already studied the Sámi people here?

– Yes, people basically come here to study the Sámi, their problems, their culture and so forth. But the Komi and Nenets are always 'on the side' … lately, people have started talking more about the small-numbered peoples [malochislennye korennye narody], but the Komi are not a small-numbered people, even though the Komi-Izhemtsy is also rather insignificant in terms of numbers and is culturally different from the Komi-Zaryan culture.

– So this is also a small-numbered people, then?

– But the thing is that it's a part of a bigger people, it's part of the Komi-Zaryan, and the republic [the Komi Republic] is rather large, and the population is large, so there are some arguments against it. But the Nenets, they're held to be a small-numbered people for some reason. Even though they have many enough, and in Yamal there are many of them, and on the Taymyr there are Nenets, and in Arkhangelsk Province there's a whole Nenets national okrug.

In fact, the Nenets are a smaller people than the Komi, not quite reaching the 50,000-member 'barrier' that the Komi have crossed.

LANGUAGE

Data on Sámi Settlement and Language Competence

In 1959, 69.9 per cent of the Russian Sámi considered Sámi to be their native language; by 1979, the percentage had fallen to 56.2. These figures were in the lower middle range compared to the other Northern Peoples, but the decline was one of the greatest (Taksami 1990a: 24).

The figures in the following table are taken from Rantala (1992: 17 and 1994a: 313), who obtained them from the Murmansk Province statistical bureau, where they were generated in 1989 as a part of the all-Soviet census. In general, these official figures as to how many Sámi speak Sámi as their mother tongue were not entirely reliable since they tended to vary. Nor did they correspond entirely to 'passport identities' as respondents were free to state different identities in the census than what was given in their passports (Simonsen 1999: 1072). These census figures are nonetheless interesting to peruse as they give an indication of the demographic situation at the early part of the period studied here.

Table 8.3. Russian Towns and Numbers of Sámi Speakers

Cities/Municipalities	Number of Sámi	Number Who Speak Sámi
Apatity	52	18
Kandalaksha	19	7
Kirovsk	12	7
Kola rayon	220	69
Kovdor rayon	107	21
Lovozero rayon	915	494
Monchegorsk	27	7
Murmansk	183	58
Olenegorsk	36	11
Pechenga	13	6
Polyarnyy	4	2
Polyarnyye Zori	7	2
Severomorsk	20	6

Table 8.3. continued

Cities/Municipalities	Number of Sámi	Number Who Speak Sámi
Terskiy	7	1
Zapolyarnyy	3	1
Total	1,625	710

Comparing these numbers to the 2002 All-Russia Census, we find that out of 1,769 people who claimed to be Sámi, 568 also said they knew the Sámi language. Furthermore, 1089 lived in rural locations, whereas 680 lived in urban areas. If we accept these data as indicating the actual change in linguistic competence, the following diagram reflects the situation. Note that between the 1989 and 2002 censuses, an increase occurred in the number of people who reported themselves to be Sámi while the number of those who reported that they could speak the language decreased.

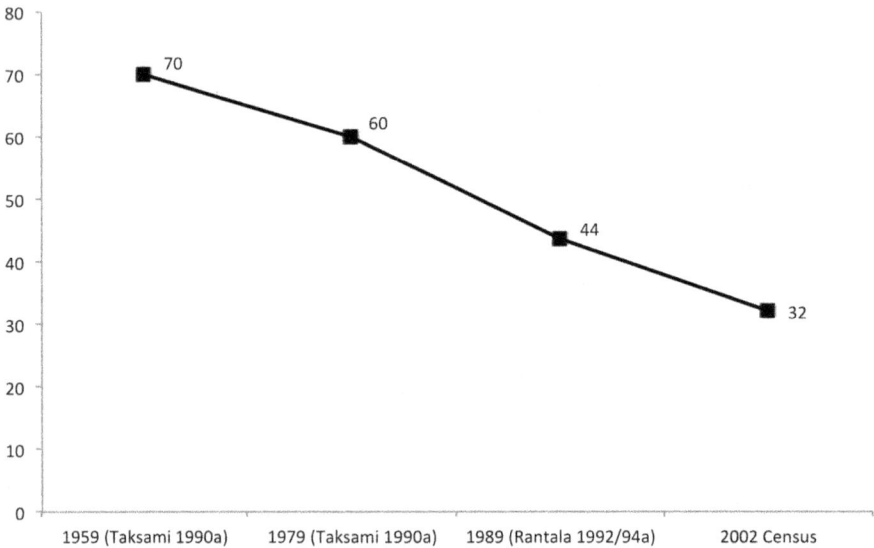

Figure 8.1. Percentage of Sámi Speakers among the Russian Sámi

Scheller's recently gathered data (2011: 86) indicate that in Russia today about 700 people have some knowledge of the Kildin Sámi language, 200 of whom are 'potential language users' and only 100 of whom are 'active speakers'. North Sámi is now the second most widespread Sámi language (around 100 say that they know some, and there are about 4 active speakers); approximately 20 people know some Ter and another 20 know some Skolt. Whereas Ter has one or two active speakers, Skolt has none. This is a fate shared by Akkala, whose situation is worse: unlike Skolt, Akkala is not native to any areas outside Russia, and in Russia there may not be anyone familiar with this language at all (Scheller 2011: 88–89).

Three Russian Sámi Alphabets

Table 8.4. Kert's Alphabet

А	Й	Р	Ш
Ä	К	Р̣	Ъ
Б	Л	Р̨	Ы
В	М̡	С	Ӹ
Г	М	Т	Ь
Д	Н	У	Ҍ
Е	Ӈ	Ӱ	Э
Ё	Ӈ	Ф	Ӭ
Ж	О	Х	Ю
З	Ö	Ц	Ц̨
И	П	Ч	

Source: Kert 1986: 9

Table 8.5. Kuruch's Alphabet

А	И	О	Ш
Ä	Й	П	Щ
Б	Ј	Р	Ъ
В	К	Р̣	Ы
Г	Л	С	Ь
Д	Л̡	Т	Ҍ
Е	М	У	Э
Ё	М̡	Ф	Ӭ
Ж	Н	Х	Ю
З	Ӈ	Ц	Ц̨
И	Ӈ	Ч	

Source: Kuruch 1985: 16

Table 8.6. Kuruch, Afanas'yeva and Vinogradova's Alphabet

А	Й	П	Щ
Ä	Ӣ	Р	Ъ
Б	К	Ҏ	Ы
В	Л	С	Ь
Г	Ӆ	Т	Ҍ
Д	М	У	Э
Е	Ӎ	Ф	Ӭ
Ё	Н	Х	Ю
Ж	Ӈ	Ц	Ц
З	Ӊ	Ч	
И	О	Ш	' [apostrophe]

Source: Kuruch, Afanas'yeva and Vinogradova 1995: 7

THREE INTERTWINED SOCIAL PROBLEMS

On two different occasions, an elderly woman from Lovozero gave her explanation of how the main social problems among the Russian Sámi community began and how they were interconnected, linking them to *ukrupneniye*.

> ... people didn't want to come here from Drozdovka, from Varzino, from Chudzyavr and other villages. ... The *kolkhoz* 'Bolshevik' over at Varzino was really rich. It wasn't bad at Chudzyavr either. But then the policy of *ukrupneniye* began ... people had to live under terrible conditions. The Sámi families were big back then. And here you have a family of 7, 8, 9, 10, and a place to live the size of my kitchen, maybe two – and that's the house. ... These problems are the basic reason for the drunkenness, and where there's drunkenness there's suicides and marriagelessness [*bezbrachiye*]. These three big problems were connected, they were very tightly connected.

> ... these suicides were connected to the fact that the entire population of our district had been moved here on the basis of a government order ... the *ukrupneniye* led to the loss of all Sámi villages – Varzino, Drozdovka and other settlements. And all those who came here ... people left their homes, left their work, and came here, to no work, and of course people started to drink, they felt terrible and started killing themselves, annihilating themselves ... and the young people stopped marrying [the interviewee uses the word *zhenitsiya* – marrying a woman – so she is here talking about the men] ... they started drinking, so they couldn't marry.

> – What about the women?

> – It was basically the men ... the women started marrying others ... Russians [*russkiye*], Ukrainians. ... And because our boys started drinking they didn't look at our girls.

> – *Why?*

> They drank ... when they start drinking, they don't think about any problems anymore, don't have to think about the future ... they drank because their parents came here from other places, and the problems came: no work, no places to live, if they wanted to get married, where would they go? Nowhere to take your family. Before, there used to be big families, many children, but where could you take another family now? And so the problems grew. First there was marriagelessness, then alcoholism and suicide. And alcoholism also led to suicide and marriagelessness.

THE COMPLEXITY OF ETHNIC IDENTITY

Regardless of the occasional remaining animosity among the groups, the Sámi identity is recognized as being highly complex, and most Sámi acknowledge a many-faceted ethnic heritage. A Sámi woman from one of the small roadless villages explained how she and her children, of an ethnically complex background, consider themselves to be Sámi.

– I consider myself purely Sámi, but I don't speak [Sámi]. … Until sixth grade I was in the tundra, but after that I wasn't in the tundra.

– And you spoke Sámi in the tundra?

– No.

– No?

– No, my mum didn't speak [Sámi]….

– She couldn't speak Sámi?

– I don't know, her mum was Russian [russkiy], our grandmother was Russian and they didn't speak together in Sámi. Grandfather was a Sámi, but grandmother was a Russian and they didn't speak Sámi together. And since mum couldn't speak it, dad therefore didn't use Sámi with her. We spoke Komi, not Sámi….

– And your husband is Komi?

– No, he's a Russian … from [a place in southern Russia].

– Do your children consider themselves Sámi?

– My children are all Sámi. … And they're all officially Sámi according to their passports. … They also understand Komi. Because their grandmother spoke Komi….

– The Russian grandmother?

– Yes, Grandmother was a Russian. She spoke Komi, I don't know why. … Maybe if we lived in [the southern birthplace of her husband], maybe then we would also be Russians. But we live here, and then it's almost as if we have to be Sámi.

Similarly, a Sámi grandmother from Lovozero detailed the ethnic background of her grandchildren, and how the end of the passport categories made it difficult to prove one's Sáminess in the absence of 'racial' traits that could support Sámi identity.

– I have two grandchildren, with six different bloodlines in them. From the mother's side it's Ukrainians, Germans, Russians [russkiye]. From the father's side it's Sámi, Komi and Nenets.

– And they'll consider themselves Sámi?

– I don't know yet.

– In the passports?

– Now we have new passports without nationalities. … The nationality won't be shown there. … I think it's a shame. … We're mixed with everyone now. And who can look at me and say that I'm a Sámi? And how should I show them that I'm a Sámi? … I can't. And how can my grandchildren show that they're [Sámi]? … I can show it, I can speak, I know the language, but they don't know the language and they're not going to. … This is very bad. We were Russian [rossiyskie] Sámi. But now we're all going to be Russians [russkiye]. … Yes, we'll be like Russians [russkiye]. Particularly those whose facial features don't show any special nationality. There are some facial features that clearly show nationality, you can look and feel that this is not the Russian nation [russkaya natsiya]. Pure Russians [russkiye … chistiye], there's none of those here now. There haven't been for a long time.

Many urban Sámi today know only indirectly about the land-based livelihoods and the tundra so symbolically important for many Russian Sámi. This Sámi girl from Murmansk became personally acquainted with these things for the first time while staying in the Nordic countries. For her, the fact that she can no longer be registered as Sámi in her passport is a great loss.

– I feel that, on the whole, I worship the tundra. … I fell in love with it in Finland … it's so beautiful, I love it more than the woods. But I guess this too just shows that I'm a Sámi.

– Do you feel like a Sámi now?

– I don't know. In principle, I would like to. …

– Your brother, I think, feels like a Sámi.

– Well, maybe I feel that way too, but I don't know if that is exactly what I feel.

– Did you have it written into your passport?

– You know, that's really a problem. We've got new passports now … and in those, they've decided not to show nationality … and I've lived all my life dreaming that I'd have it written there …

Note

1. Osherenko et al. (1997: 35) and Vakhtin (1994: 34) give similar figures, but with some minor variations (possibly due to error) which have been omitted here.

BIBLIOGRAPHY

All names in the bibliography are given here as in the original. Where they vary due to diverging transliteration systems applied in the different sources, for example 'Kiselev' and 'Kiseljov', the other form follows in square brackets.

Ainana, L., N. Mymrin, O. Veter and L. Bogoslovskaya (1997) *Role of the Eskimo Society of Chukotka in Encouraging Traditional Native Use of Wildlife Resources by Chukotka Natives and in Conducting Shore Based Observations on the Distribution of Bowhead Whales, Balaena Mysticetus, in Coastal Waters off the South-Eastern Part of the Chukotka Peninsula,* Barrow: Department of Wildlife Management.

Alekseyeva, A. (1981) 'Saamskaya grammatika', *Polyarnaya pravda,* 10 November, p. 4.

Alekseyeva, A. (1989) 'Esli budet silen malen'kiy narod', *Polyarnaya pravda,* 8 September, p. 3.

Alekseyeva, A. (1997) 'Istoriya o tom kak amerikanets nakazal Lovozero na million dollarov', *Lovozerskaya pravda,* 4 April, p. 3.

Alymov, V. (1925) 'Ob assimilatsii loparey', *Vestnik karelo-murmanskogo kraya,* (17–18): 7–10.

Anderson, B. (1983/1991) *Imagined Communities: Reflections on the Origin and Spread of Nationalism,* London: Verso.

Andreassen, N. (1997) 'Nashi i ne nashi', *Murmanskiy vestnik,* 25 September, p. 2.

Andreassen, N. (1998) 'Syomga – k stolu, reka – k gibeli', *Murmanskiy vestnik,* 6 May, p. 3.

Antonova, A. (1982) *Sam' bukvarr',* Leningrad: Prosveshchsheniye.

Antonova, A. (1988/1996) 'A Saami Woman's Letter to the Central Authorities of the RSFSR', in A. Pika, J. Dahl and I. Larsen (eds) *Anxious North: Indigenous Peoples in Soviet and Post-Soviet Russia: Selected Documents, Letters and Articles,* Copenhagen: IWGIA, pp. 171–183.

Antonova, A. (1992) 'Hvor står vi samer i dag?', *Ságat,* 11 January.

Antonova, A. (1997) 'Prezidentu – rodnoy yazyk?', *Lovozerskaya pravda,* 24 January, p. 2.

Antonova, A., G. Lukin, P. Fefelov, N. Milyutina, G. Denisova, I. Galkin and E. Yulin (1997) 'Park "Khibiny" – saamskiy?', *Lovozerskaya pravda,* 29 August, p. 5.

Antonova, A. and L. Sashenkova (1998) 'Ne meshayte 'Tundre"', *Lovozerskaya pravda,* 24 April, p. 1.

Arevkova, L.T. (1988) 'Ekonomicheskoye i sotsial'noye razvitiye', in E.N. Frolova (ed.) *Murmanskoy oblasti 50 let,* Murmansk: Murmanskoye knizhnoye izdatel'stvo, pp. 71–152.

Argyle, W.J. (1976) 'Size and Scale as Factors in the Development of Nationalist Movements', in A.D. Smith (ed.) *Nationalist Movements,* London: Macmillan, pp. 31–53.

Arvola, E. (1990) 'Na vzglyad norvezhtsev', *Polyarnaya pravda,* 24 January, p. 4.

Avdeyeva, L. (1997) 'Saamskaya kul'tura v Rossii', *Zhivaya Arktika,* 8(3):8.

Avdeyeva, L.P., A.A. Antonova and E.N Kirillov (1998) 'Obrashcheniye: Ot imeni uchreditel'noy konferentsii saamov murmanskoy oblasti', *Lovozerskaya pravda,* 31 July, p. 5.

Barnes, J.A. (1979) *Who Should Know What? Social Science, Privacy and Ethics,* Harmondsworth: Penguin.

Beach, H. (1988) *The Saami of Lapland,* London: Minority Rights Group [Report 55].

Beach, H. (1992) 'Reindeer Herding on the Kola Peninsula – Report of a Visit with Saami Herders of Sovkhoz Tundra', in R. Kvist (ed.) *Readings in Saami History, Culture and Language III,* Umeå: Centre for Arctic Cultural Research, pp. 113–142.

Beach, H. (1994) 'The Saami of Lapland', in Minority Rights Group (ed.) *Polar Peoples: Self-Determination and Development,* London: Minority Rights Publications, pp. 147–205.

Beach, H. and M. Anderson (1992) 'Saami', in L. Bennett (ed.) *Encyclopedia of World Cultures,* Vol. IV, pp. 220–223.

Belyayev, O. (1988) 'Tayna svyashchennykh ozyor', *Polyarnaya pravda,* 29 April, p. 4.

Belyayeva, L.S. (1991) *Saamskaya etnopedagogika,* Murmansk: Murmanskiy gosudarstvennyy pedagogicheskiy institut.

Berg, B.A. (2000) 'Mot en korporativ reindrift. Samisk reindrift i det 20. århundre – eksemplifisert gjennom studier av reindriften på Helgeland' *Dieđut,* No 3, Guovdageaidnu/Kautokeino: Sámi Instituhtta.

Berg-Nordlie, M. (2011a) 'Need and Misery in the Eastern Periphery: Nordic Sámi Media Debate on the Kola Sámi', *Acta Borealia,* 28(1):19–36.

Berg-Nordlie, M. (2011b) 'Striving to Unite. The Russian Sámi and the Nordic Sámi Parliament Model', *Arctic Review on Law and Politics,* 2(1):52–176.

Berg-Nordlie, M. (2012) 'The Iron Curtain through Sápmi. Pan-Sámi Politics, Nordic Cooperation and the Russian Sámi', *Humanistica Oerebroensia, L'Image du Sápmi,* 2:436–459.

Berg-Nordlie, M. and A. Schou (2011) 'Who are Indigenous – and How Should it Matter? Discourses on Indigenous Rights in Norway and Nepal', *Ethnopolitics Papers,* November, 13:1–31.

Binn, C. (1987) 'The Study of Soviet and East European Elites', in G. Moyser and M. Wagstaffe (eds) *Research Methods for Elite Studies,* London: Allen & Unwin, pp. 217–231.

Bjørklund, I. (1994) 'Sámi Livelihood: Indigenous Resource Management in a Changing World', in a special issue of *Dieđut: Majority–Minority Relations: The Case of the Sámi in Scandinavia, Conference Report Guovdageaidnu, Norway, 2–4 July 1993,* (1):70–74.

Bjørklund, I. and T. Brantenberg (1981) *Samisk reindrift – norske inngrep: Om Altaelva, reindrift og Samisk kultur,* Oslo: Universitetsforlaget.

Blakkisrud, H. (1997) *Den russiske føderasjonen i støpeskjeen: etniske og territorielle utfordringer,* Oslo: Spartacus.

Bogdanov, N. (1997) 'I vsye-taki – 'Seydozero!'', *Lovozerskaya pravda,* 24 October, p. 3.

Bogdanov, V. (1997) 'Prilipaly', *Lovozerskaya pravda,* 24 October, p. 6.

Bol'shakova, N. (1997a) 'Khibiny – kolybel' tsivilizatsii', *Zhivaya Arktika,* 8(3):2.

Bol'shakova, N. (1997b) 'Natsional'ny park. No pochemu – "Khibiny?"', *Lovozerskaya pravda,* 29 August, p. 5.

Bol'shakova, N. (1997c) 'Rovesnik veka', *Lovozerskaya pravda,* 6 September, p. 3.

Bol'shakova, N. (1997d) 'Syna Noya zvali ne Sim, a Saam', *Murmanskiy vestnik,* 23 August, p. 5.

Borovaya, Z. (1998) 'Vystreli v tundre', *Murmanskiy vestnik,* 31 October, pp. 1–2.

Brantenberg, O.T. (1985) 'The Alta-Kautokeino Conflict, Saami Reindeer Herding and Ethnopolitics', in J. Brøsted et al. (eds) *Native Power: The Quest for Autonomy and Nationhood of Indigenous Peoples,* Oslo: Universitetsforlaget, pp. 23–48.

Brass, P.R. (1992) 'Language and National Identity in the Soviet Union and India', in A.J. Motyl (ed.) *Thinking Theoretically About Soviet Nationalities: History and Comparison in the Study of the USSR,* New York: Columbia University Press, pp. 99–128.

Brylyova, Z. (1990) 'Pravda o Komi-Izhemtsakh?', *Lovozerskaya pravda,* 20 September, p. 2.

Brylyova, Z.I. (1996) 'The History of the Kola Peninsular Komi-Izhemets', in I. Seurujärvi-Kari and U.M. Kulonen (eds) *Essays on Indigenous Identity and Rights,* Helsinki: Helsinki University Press, pp. 157–169.

Burg, S.L. (1990) 'Nationality Elites and Political Change in the Soviet Union', in L. Hadja and M. Beissinger (eds) *The Nationalities Factor in Soviet Politics and Society,* Boulder: Westview Press, pp. 24–42.

Burger, J. (1987) *Report from the Frontier: The State of the World's Indigenous Peoples,* London: Zed Books.

Burgess, R.G. (1995) *In the Field,* London: Routledge.

Calhoun, C. (1997) *Nationalism,* Buckingham: Open University Press.

Capron, A.M. (1982) 'Is Consent Always Necessary in Social Science Research?', in T. Beauchamp, R. Faden, J. Wallace and L. Walters (eds) *Ethical Issues in Social Science Research,* Baltimore: John Hopkins University Press, pp. 215–231.

Castrén, M.A. (1852) *Reseminnen från åren 1838–1844,* Helsingfors.

Cherkasskiy, Ya. (1998) 'Vernis' k saamam svashchennyy myandash', *Murmanskiy vestnik,* 18 July, p. 3.

Chernyakov, Z.Ye. (1933) *Saam bukvar,* Moscow: Nauchno-isslodovatel'skaya assotsiatsiya instituta narodov severa TsIK SSSR.

CIMN (2011a) 'Kratkaya informatsiya ob obshchestvennykh organizatsii, obshchinakh, natsional'nykh predpriyatiyakh'. Retrieved 19 August 2011 from http//www.gov-murman.ru/natpers/orgz.

CIMN (2011b) 'Sovet predstaviteley korennykh malochislennykh narodov Severa pri Pravitel'stve Murmanskoy oblasti & Kratkaya informatsiya ob obshchestvennykh organizatsiyakh, obshchinakh, natsional'nykh prepriyatiyakh'. Retrieved 19 August 2011 from http//www.gov-murman.ru/natpers/orgz/#2 and http//www.gov-murman.ru/natpers/orgz/#2.

Coakley, J. (1992) 'The Social Origins of Nationalist Movements and Explanations of Nationalism: A Review', in J. Coakley (ed.) *The Social Origins of Nationalist Movements,* London: Sage, pp. 1–20.

Connor, W. (1992) 'The Nation and its Myth', in A.D. Smith (ed.) *Ethnicity and Nationalism,* Leiden: E.J. Brill, pp. 48–57.

Corbett, H. (1996) 'The Rights of Indigenous Peoples: A Comparison of the Rights of Saami and Aboriginal Peoples in Australia', in I. Seurujärvi-Kari and U.M. Kulonen (eds) *Essays on Indigenous Identity and Rights,* Helsinki: Helsinki University Press, pp. 40–65.

Cramér, T. (1994) 'Sámi Legal Rights Cleansing in Scandinavia', *Indigenous Affairs,* (3):53–55.

Dallmann, W. K. (1997) *Indigenous Peoples of the Northern Part of the Russian Federation and their Environment, INSROP Working Paper,* No. 90, Oslo: Fridtjof Nansen Institute.

Dallmann, W.K. and G. Diachkova (1999) 'Indigenous Ethnic Groups of the North, Siberia and the Far East of the Russian Federation. Part I: The Northern Zone – Kola to Kamchatka', in W. Dallmann (ed.) *NNSIPRA Bulletin,* (3):15–31.

Doiban, V.A., M. Pretes and A.V. Sekarev (1992) 'Economic Development in the Kola Region, USSR: An Overview', *Polar Record,* 28(164):7–16.

Eek, A. (1984) 'Probleme der Lappischen Sprache und Kultur auf der Konferenz in Lujavr', *Sovetskoye finno-ugrovedeniye,* 20(3):237–240.

Eek, A. and R.D. Kuruch (1983) 'Acoustic Measurements of some Quantity Patterns in Kildin Lapp', *Sovetskoye finno-ugrovedeniye,* 19(1):16–22.

Eidheim, H. (1985) 'Indigenous Peoples and the State: The Saami Case and Norway', J. Brøsted et al. (eds) *Native Power: The Quest of Indigenous Peoples for Autonomy and Nationhood,* Oslo: Universitetsforlaget, pp. 155–171.

Endyukovskiy, A.G. (1937) 'Saamskiy (loparskiy) yazyk', *Yazyk i pis'mennost' narodov Severa,* 1:125–162.

Eriksen, T.H. (1993a) 'The Epistemological Status of the Concept of Ethnicity', *The Anthropology of Ethnicity Conference,* Amsterdam, December 1993.

Eriksen, T.H. (1993b) *Ethnicity and Nationalism: Anthropological Perspectives,* London: Pluto.

Eriksson, J. (1997) *Partition and Redemption: A Machiavellian Analysis of Sami and Basque Patriotism,* Umeå: Umeå University.

Ersson, B. and B. Hedin (1977) *Sa'mit: Samerna – Nordkalottens folk,* Stockholm: LTs förlag.

Fedorov, P. and A. Sinitskiy (1998) 'Yeshcho raz o demografii', *Polyarnaya pravda,* 29 December, p. 2.

Filippov, V. (1990) 'Nasha zemlya: Na dele proyavlyat' sabotu ob uklade zhizni korennogo naseleniya Zapolyar'ya', *Polyarnaya pravda,* 10 January, p. 4.

Finnish Sámi Parliament (2007) 'Saamelaisten lukumäärä vuoden 2007 Saamelaiskäräjävaaleissa'. Retrieved 16 August 2011 from http//www.samediggi. fi/index.php?option=com_docman&task=cat_view&gid=114&Itemid=10.

Fondahl, G.A. (1995) 'The Status of the Indigenous Peoples in the Russian North', *Post-Soviet Geography,* 36(4):215–224.

Fryer, P. (1998) *Elites, Language and Education in the Komi Ethnic Revival,* Cambridge: Scott Polar Research Institute, University of Cambridge [unpublished Ph.D. thesis].

Galkin, I.M. (1997a) 'Ekho konferentsii na Seyde. Ne speshite aplodiravat', *Lovozerskaya pravda*, 29 April, p. 2.

Galkin, I. (1997b) '"Giperborea – 97": versii podtverdilis', *Lovozerskaya pravda*, 29 August, p. 5.

Galliher, J.F. (1973) 'The Protection of Human Subjects: A Re-Examination of the Professional Code of Ethics', *American Sociologist*, 8(August):93–100.

Gellner, E. (1992) 'Nationalism in the Vacuum', in A.J. Motyl (ed.) *Thinking Theoretically About Soviet Nationalities: History and Comparison in the Study of the USSR*, New York: Columbia University Press, pp. 243–254.

Geographical (1998) 'Fighting Spirit', *Geographical*, 70(10):52–53.

Golovnev, A.V. (1997) 'Indigenous Leadership in North-Western Siberia: Traditional Patterns and their Contemporary Manifestations', *Arctic Anthropology*, 34(1):149–166.

Gramsci, A. (2001) 'The Formation of Intellectuals', in V. Leitch (ed.) *Norton Anthology of Theory and Criticism*, New York: Norton, pp. 1135–1143.

Hætta, O.M. (1993) *The Sámi: Indigenous People of the Arctic*, Karasjok: Davvi girji.

Hætta, O.M. (1994) *Samene: historie, kultur, samfunn*, Oslo: Grøndahl og Dreyers forlag.

Hallström, G. (1911) 'Kolalapparnas hotade existens', *Ymer*, 31(3):239–316.

Hansen, E. (1998) *Living Conditions on the Kola Peninsula* [FAFO Report 155], Oslo: FAFO-SOTECO.

Hansen, L.I. (2004) 'Siida', in I. Imsen and H. Winge (eds) *Norsk historisk leksikon*, 2nd ed. Oslo: Cappelen Akademisk Forlag.

Hansen, L.I. and B. Olsen (2004) *Samenes Historie fram til 1750*, Tromsø: Cappelen Akademisk Forlag.

Haruchi, G. (2002) 'The Indigenous Intelligentsia', in T. Køhler and K. Wessendorf (eds) *Towards a New Millennium. Ten Years of the Indigenous Movement in Russia*, IWGIA Document No. 107, Copenhagen, pp. 86–93.

Hechter, M. (1986) 'Theories of Ethnic Relations', in J.F. Stack (ed.) *The Primordial Challenge: Ethnicity in the Contemporary World*, New York: Greenwood Press, pp. 13–24.

Helander, E. (1994) 'The Sámi People: Demographics, Origin, Economy, Culture', in a special issue of *Die ut: Majority–Minority Relations: The Case of the Sámi in Scandinavia, Conference Report Guovdageaidnu, Norway, 2–4 July 1993*, (1):23–34.

Henriksen, G. (1985) 'Anthropologists as Advocates: Promoters of Pluralism or Makers of Clients?', in R. Paine (ed.) *Advocacy and Anthropology, First Encounters*, St. John's: Institute of Social and Economic Research, Memorial University of Newfoundland, pp. 119–129.

Henriksen, G. (1986) *Statlig kontroll og samisk reaksjon: En rapport fra H.land*, Bergen: Sosialantropologisk institutt.

Henriksen, G. (1991) 'The Experience of Social Worth as a Force in Inter-Ethnic Relations', in G. Haaland, R. Grønhaug and G. Henriksen (eds) *The Ecology of Choice and Symbol: Essays in Honour of Fredrik Barth*, Bergen: Alma Mater, pp. 407–425.

Henriksen, J. (1996) 'The Legal Status of Saamiland Rights in Finland, Russia, Norway and Sweden', *Indigenous Affairs*, 2:4–13.

Henriksen, J. (1998) 'Strengthening Sámi Cross Boundary Institutions and Relations', *Indigenous Affairs*, 3:34–39.

Hirsti, R. (1974) *Suenjel-folket ved veis ende*, Oslo: Tiden Norsk Forlag.

Hobsbawm, E. (1990) *Nations and Nationalism since 1780: Programme, Myth, Reality*, Cambridge: Cambridge University Press.

Hønneland, G. (1997) 'Integrasjon vs. atuonomi: En tilnærming til sivil–militære forhold i Russland', *Nordisk Østforum*, 11(3):37–49.

Hønneland, G. and A.K. Jørgensen (1998) 'Closed Cities on the Kola Peninsula: From Autonomy to Integration?', *Polar Geography*, 22(4):231–248.

Hønneland, G. and A.K. Jørgensen (1999) *Integration vs. Autonomy: Civil–Military Relations on the Kola Peninsula*, Aldershot: Ashgate.

Humphrey, C. (1991) '"Icebergs", Barter, and the Mafia in Provincial Russia', *Anthropology Today*, 7(2):8–13.

Humphrey, C. (1995) 'Introduction', *Cambridge Anthropology*, 18(2):1–11.

Humphrey, C. (1998) 'The Domestic Mode of Production in Post-Soviet Siberia?', *Anthropology Today*, 14(3):2–8.

Ingold, T. (1976) *The Skolt Lapps Today*, Cambridge: Cambridge University Press.

Itkonen, T. I. (1958) *Koltan ja Kuolanlapin sanakirja*, Helsinki: Suomalais-Ugrilainen seura.

Ivanov-Dyatlov, F. G. (1928) *Nablyudeniya vracha na Kol'skom Poluostrove*, Leningrad: Gosudarstvennoye russkoye geograficheskoe obshchestvo.

IWGIA (1990) 'Indigenous Peoples of the Soviet North', Document No. 67, Copenhagen.

Janhunen, J. (1991) 'Ethnic Death and Survival in the Soviet North', *Journal de la Société Finno-Ougrienne*, 83:111–122.

Jillker, G. (1994a) 'Parlamentetet förvantas att få lagstiftande makt', *Samefolket*, 75(8):18.

Josefsen, E. (2007) 'Samene og de nasjonale parlamentene – kanaler for politisk innflytelse', *Gáldu Čála – Tidsskrift for urfolksrettigheter*, 2:1–28.

Kalstad, J.A. (2006) 'Gi oss tilbake vårt beiteland' – samisk reindrift på Kolahalvøya', in *Ottar* No. 1: *Reindrift i endring*, Tromsø: Tromsø Museum – Universitetsmuseet, Universitetet i Tromsø.

Kalstad, J.A. (2009) *Dorogoy Nadezhd. Politika Rossyskogo gosudarstva i polozhenie saamskogo naroda v Rossii (1864–2003)*, trans. I.B. Tsirkunov. Murmansk: Murmanskoe knizhnoye izdatel'stvo.

Kaminsky, V.I. (1996) 'Medical Care of the Indigenous Peoples in the Lovozero County', in I. Seurujärvi-Kari and U.M. Kulonen (eds) *Essays on Indigenous Identity and Rights*, Helsinki: Helsinki University Press, pp. 149–156.

Karlov, V.V. (1991) 'Narodnosti Severa Sibiri: osobennosti vosproizvodstva i al'ternativy razvitiya', *Sovetskaya etnografiya*, 5(Sept.–Oct.):3–16.

Kelman, H.C. (1982) 'Ethical Issues in Different Social Science Methods', in T. Beauchamp, R. Faden, J. Wallace and L. Walters (eds) *Ethical Issues in Social Science Research*, Baltimore: John Hopkins University Press, pp. 40–98.

Kert, G.M. (1966) 'Saamskiy yazyk', *Jazyki narodov SSSR*, 3:155–171.

Kert, G.M. (1971) *Saamskiy yazyk: fonetika, morfologiya, sintaks*, Leningrad: Nauka.

Kert, G.M. (1972) 'På leting etter samenes opprinnelse', *Sovjetnytt*, 29 April, p. 1.

Kert, G.M. (1986) *Slovar', saamsko-russkiy i russko-saamskiy*, Leningrad: Prosveshchenie.

Kharuzin, N. (1890) *Russkiye lopari: Ocherki proshlogo i sovremennogo byta*, Moscow: no publisher.

Khazanov, A. (1995) *After the USSR: Ethnicity, Nationalism and Politics in the Commonwealth of Independent States*, Madison: Wisconsin University Press.

Kiselev, A.A. [also Kiseljov] (1988) 'Mesto na karte', in E.N. Frolova (ed.) *Murmanskoy oblasti 50 let,* Murmansk: Murmanskoye knizhnoye izdatel'stvo, pp. 5–12.

Kiselev, A. [also Kiseljov] (1994a) 'Murmanskiye Komi [1]', *Lovozerskaya pravda,* 5 August, p. 4.

Kiselev, A. [also Kiseljov] (1994b) 'Murmanskiye Komi [2]', *Lovozerskaya pravda,* 8 August, p. 3.

Kiselev, A. [also Kiseljov] (1994c) 'Murmanskiye Komi [3]', *Lovozerskaya pravda,* 12 August, p. 4.

Kiselev, A. [also Kiseljov] (1994d) 'Murmanskiye Komi [4]', *Lovozerskaya pravda,* 19 August, p. 3.

Kiselev, A. [also Kiseljov] (1997) 'Ot gubernii – k okrugu', *Murmanskiy vestnik,* 21 August, p. 3.

Kiselev, A.A. and T.A. Kiseleva [also Kiseljov and Kiseljova] (1979a) *Sovetskiye saamy: istoriya, ekonomika, kul'tura,* Murmansk: Murmanskoye knizhnoye izdatel'stvo.

Kiselev, A.A. and T.A. Kiseleva [also Kiseljov and Kiseljova] (1979b) 'Kul'turnaya revolyutsiya v tundra', *Lovozerskaya pravda,* 3 February, p. 2.

Kiselev, A.A. and T.A. Kiseleva [also Kiseljov and Kiseljova] (1979c) 'Kul'turnaya revolyutsiya v tundra', *Lovozerskaya pravda,* 6 February, p. 2.

Kiseleva, T.A. [also Kiseljov and Kiseljova] (1994) 'Vliyaniye sotsial'no-eknomicheskikh faktorov na razvitiye olenevodstva kol'skogo poluostrova v 1900–1980-e gody', in L.N. Pod'yelskaya (ed.) *Voprosy istorii evropeyskogo Severa,* Petrozavodsk: Izdatel'stvo Petrozavodskogo Universiteta, pp. 72–77.

Kiseljov, A. and T. Kiseljova [also Kiselev and Kiseleva] (1981) *Samerna i Sovjetunionen: historia, näringsliv, kultur,* Lund: Lunds geografiska institut.

Klaus, V. (1987) 'Saamsko-russkiy slovar'…' [book review], *Sovetskoye finno-ugrovedeniye,* 22(2):145–149.

KNSS (2010) 'Resheniye Vtorogo S''yezda saamov Murmanskogo oblasti – saami'. Retrieved 19 August 2011 from http://saamisups.ucoz.ru/publ/vtoroj_sezd_saamov_murmanskoj_oblasti/reshenie/4-1-0-.

Kobelev, A., O. Andreyeva, N. Groshev, H. Dodonova and Yu. Budylev (1998) 'V zashchitu olenykh pastbishch' [letter to the State Duma, the Federal Council (Sovet Federatsii) and the newspapers *Sovetskaya Rossi* and *Veteran*], *Lovozerskaya pravda,* 2 October, p. 2.

Kolpakova, E. (1991) 'Na konferentsii kol'skikh saamov', *Lovozerskaya pravda,* 28 September, pp. 2, 4.

Konakov, N.D., O.V. Kotov and Yu. G. Rochev (1984) *Izhemskiye Komi na Kol'skom Poluostrove,* Syktyvkar: Akademiya nauk.

Koneva, N. (1971) 'Svetlyy put' – rasskaz Petra Ivanovicha Terent'yeva, odnogo iz lovozerskikh khodokov', *Polyarnaya pravda,* 19 April, p. 2.

Konopatov, Yu. P. (1997) 'Nam koshchunstva ne prostyat', *Lovozerskaya pravda,* 26 September, p. 3.

Konstantinov, Yu. (1996) 'Field Research of Reindeer-Herding in the Kola Peninsula: Problems and Challenges', *Acta Borealia,* (2):53–68.

Konstantinov, Yu. (1997) 'Memory of Lenin Ltd. Reindeer-Herding Brigades of the Kola Peninsula', *Anthropology Today,* 13(3):14–19.

Konstantinov, Yu. (1999) *The Northern Sea Route and Local Communities in Northwest Russia: Social Impact Assessment for the Murmansk Region, INSROP Working Paper,* No. 152, Oslo: The Fridtjof Nansen Institute.

Konstantinov, Yu. (2011): 'Premonitions of Change: Luujäu'rr (Lovozero) Home Talk Twenty Years After', in T. Mustonen and K. Mustonen (eds) *Eastern Sámi Atlas,* Vaasa: Oy Fram Ab, pp. 192–198.

Kotov, O.V. (1987) *Ethnicheskoye samosoznaniye kol'skikh Komi,* Syktyvkar: Akademiya nauk.

Krupnik, I. (1993) *Arctic Adaptations,* Hanover: University Press of New England.

Krupnik, I. and N. Vakhtin (1997) 'Indigenous Knowledge in Modern Culture: Siberian Yupik Ecological Legacy in Transition', in *Arctic Anthropology,* 34(1):236–252.

Kuimova, T. (1990) 'Na putakh vozrozhdeniya', *Lovozerskaya pravda,* 27 October, p. 2.

Kumunzhiyeva, M. (1997) 'Kolbasa baran'ya gumanitarnaya', *Lovozerskaya pravda,* 13 June, p. 4.

Kuoljok, K.E. (1985) *The Revolution in the North: Soviet Ethnography and Nationality Policy,* Uppsala: Almqvist & Wiksell.

Kuropyatnik, M.S. (1992) 'Local Variants of Functioning of the Kola Saami Community', *Specimina Sibirica,* 5:163–168.

Kuruch, R.D. (ed.) (1985) *Saamsko-russkiy slovar': Sam-rush soagknehk,* Moscow: Russkiy yazyk.

Kuruch, R.D., N.E. Afanas'yeva and I.V. Vinogradova (1995) *Pravila orfografiy i punktuaktsiy saamskogo yazyka,* Murmansk: Murmanskiy sektor lingvisticheskikh problem finno-ugorskikh narodnostey Kraynogo Severa.

Kuznetsova, A. (1989) 'Utverzhdat' kul'turu naroda', *Lovozerskaya pravda,* 23 May, p. 1.

Kuznetsova, A. (1991) 'Posle kontserta … v raysovete', *Lovozerskaya pravda,* 16 February, p. 2

Kuznetsova, A. (1997a) 'Metamorfoza – ili kak uchilishche stalo filialom', *Lovozerskaya pravda,* 14 February, p. 2.

Kuznetsova, A. (1997b) 'Na grani sryva', *Lovozerskaya pravda,* 18 April, p. 5.

Kuznetsova, A. (1997c) 'Priroda i chelovek: "Khibiny – svoimi glazami"', *Lovozerskaya pravda,* 13 June, p. 3.

Kuznetsova, A. (1997d) 'Budut delit', *Lovozerskaya pravda,* 29 August, p. 1.

Kuznetsova, A. (1998) '"Tundra" – vremya obnovleniya', *Lovozerskaya pravda,* 29 May, pp. 1, 6.

Kuznetsova, A. (1999) 'Oosmovtsy v kommune', *Lovozerskaya pravda,* 12 February, p. 1.

Larsson-Kalvemo, A. (1995) *'Fighting for Survival' – Överlevelsesstrategier i nya omständigheter bland samerna på Kolahalvön,* Tromsø: Seksjon for Samiske studier, Universitetet i Tromsø [unpublished Master's thesis].

Lasko, L.N. [also Lasku] and G. Osherenko (1999) *The Sámi People and the Northern Sea Route: Juridical, Social and Cultural Concerns, INSROP Working Paper,* No. 154, Oslo: The Fridtjof Nansen Institute.

Lazarev, E.E. and E.J. Patsija (1991) 'Sociala aspekter på de kolska samernas livsföring', in M. Aikio and K. Korpijaakko (eds) *Samesymposium,* Rovaniemi: University of Lapland.

Leinonen, M. (2008) 'The Filmans. Nomads at a Dead End', *Journal of Northern Studies,* (2):51–75.

Lindgren, E.J. (1977) 'The Skolt Lapps Today' [book review of T. Ingold (1976) *The Skolt Lapps Today,* Cambridge: Cambridge University Press], *British Book News,* June, p. 494.

Lobanov, A. (1991) 'Konferentsiya saamov: "Dayte nam zhit po-svoyemu..."', *Polyarnaya pravda,* 20 September, p. 1.

Lobanov, A. (1992) '"Kogo khochu – togo lyublyu", otvetil na setovaniya rabotnitsy zagsa modoy saam', *Polyarnaya pravda,* 11 February, p. 3.

Loginova, G. (1998a) '"Laplandskaya initsiativa" rodom iz Germanii', *Polyarnaya pravda,* 22 April, p. 2.

Loginova, G. (1998b) 'Saamy i nemtsy – sosedi po Vselennoy', *Polyarnaya pravda,* 30 October, p. 1.

Luk'yanchenko, T.V. [also Lukantschenko] (1994) 'Promyslovoye khozyaystvo saamov Kol'skogo Poluostrova v sovremennykh usloviyakh razvivayushchikhsya rynochnykh otnosheniy', in Z.P. Sokolova (ed.) *Narody Severa i Sibiri v usloviyakh reform i demokraticheskikh preobrazavaniy,* Moscow: Institut etnologii i antropologii im. N.N. Miklukho-Maklaya Rossiskoy akademii nauk, pp. 50–63.

Magga, O.H. (1994) 'The Policy Towards the Sámi People in Norway', in a special issue of *Diedut* (1994) *Majority–Minority Relations: The Case of the Sámi in Scandinavia, Conference Report Guovdageaidnu, Norway, 2–4 July 1993,* (1):44–49.

Magga, O.H. (2002) 'Samisk språk – en oversikt' i Nordiska Ministerråder och Nordiska Rådet', *Samiska i ett nytt årtusande,* København: ANP.

Makseyeva, Y. (1999) 'V Lovozere shamany koldovali', *Murmanskiy Vestnik,* 9 February, p. 1.

McDonald, M. (1989) *We Are Not French!': Language, Culture and Identity in Brittany,* London: Routledge.

Medhurst, K. and G. Moyser (1987) 'Studying a Religious Elite: The Case of the Anglican Episcopate', in G. Moyser and M. Wagstaffe (eds) *Research Methods for Elite Studies,* London: Allen & Unwin, pp. 89–108.

Mikhnyak, T. (1993) 'Chtoby sokhranit' samobytnost", *Lovozerskaya pravda,* 10 December, pp. 2, 4.

Minde, H. (2003) 'The Challenge of Indigeneism. The Struggle for Sámi Land Rights and Self-Government in Norway 1960–1990', in S. Jentoft, H. Mindeand and R. Nilsen (eds) *Indigenous peoples. Resource Management and Global Rights,* Tromsø: Eburon Academic, pp. 75–107.

Minde, H. (2005) 'Assimilation of the Sami – Implementation and Consequences', *Gáldu Čála Journal of Indigenous Studies,* 3:1–34.

Minogue, K. and B. Williams (1992) 'Ethnic Conflict in the Soviet Union: The Revenge of Particularism', in A.J. Motyl (ed.) *Thinking Theoretically About Soviet Nationalities: History and Comparison in the Study of the USSR,* New York: Columbia University Press, pp. 225–242.

MSPU (2011) 'Stranitsy istorii MGPU'. Retrieved 19 August 2011 from http//www.mspu.edu.ru/index.php?option=com_content&task=category&sectionid=4&id=42&Itemid=605.

Mustonen, T. and K. Mustonen (2011) *Eastern Sámi Atlas,* Vaasa: Oy Fram Ab.

Nickel, K.P. (1994) *Samisk gramatikk,* 2nd printing, Kárášjohka: Davvi Girji o.s.

Nilsen, T. and N. Bøhmer (1994) *Sources of Radioactive Contamination in Murmansk and Arkhangel'sk County,* Oslo: Bellona.

NINA (1996) 'Sjøvandrende laksefisk på Kola', Tromsø: Norsk Institutt for naturforskning, Avdeling for arktisk økologi.

Nistad, B. (2004) *Russisk politisk idéhistorie fra opplysningstiden til idag,* Oslo: Solum.

Nordic Cooperation on Sámi Issues (2000) 'Nordisk fellesmøte – 02.11.00. Nordisk samarbeid om samiske saker' [Meeting protocol], Karasjok.

Nordic Sámi Institute (2005) 'Hvor mange snakker samisk?' Retrieved 16 April 2010 from http//www.sami-statistics.info/default.asp?nc=6253&id=46.

Nordisk sameråd (1987) 'Samernas XIII konferens. Are 13–15.08.1986. Skandinavisk upplaga' [Conference proceedings], Utsjoki: Nordisk Sameråd.

Norwegian Sámi Parliament (2011) 'Sámedikki jienastuslohku – loahpalaš listu'. Retrieved 19 August 2011 from http//samediggi.no/Artikkel.aspx?AId=2962& back=1&MId1=1&MId2=1707&MId3=2945& –.

Nuttall, M. (1998) *Protecting the Arctic. Indigenous Peoples and Cultural Survival,* Amsterdam: Harwood Academic.

Nystad, A. (1999) *Notat om urfolksamarbeidet i den Euro-Arktiske Barentsregionen,* Kirkenes: Barentssekretariatet.

OOSMO, Pravleniye (1998) 'Izbrali pravleniye', *Lovozerskaya pravda,* 30 October, p. 5.

Oresheta, M. (1996) 'Umchi menya, olen', *Polyarnaya pravda,* 28 November, p. 2.

Orgkomitet (1989) 'Assotsiatsiya kol'skikh saamov: Ustav Assotsiatii kol'skikh saamov', *Lovozerskaya pravda,* 9 September, pp. 3, 4.

Osherenko, G., D.L. Schindler, A.I. Pika and D. Bogoyavlensky (1997) *The Northern Sea Route and Native Peoples: Lessons from the 20th Century for the 21st, INSROP Working Paper,* No. 93, Oslo: The Fridjof Nansen Institute.

Otnes, P. (1970) *Den samiske nasjon,* Oslo: Pax forlag.

Paine, R. (1982) *Dam a River, Damn a People? Saami (Lapp) Livelihood and the Alta/ Kautokeino Hydro-Electric Project and the Norwegian Parliament,* Copenhagen: IWGIA [Document No. 45].

Pan'shina, N. (1995) 'Saamy, tsigane i drugiye…', *Polyarnaya pravda,* 1 March, p. 2.

Patsiya, E. (1974) 'Unikal'naya kollektsiya', *Polyarnaya pravda,* 24 November, p. 4.

Pearson, D. (1988) 'From Communality to Ethnicity: Some Theoretical Considerations on the Maori Ethnic Revival', *Ethnic and Racial Studies,* 11(2):168–191.

Pedersen, S. (1996) 'Saami Rights: A Historical and Contemporary Outlook', in I. Seurujärvi-Kari and U.M. Kulonen (eds), *Essays on Indigenous Identity and Rights,* Helsinki: Helsinki University Press, pp. 66–86.

Plyukhin, V. (1986) 'Uroki samobytnosti: Stali talismanami', *Lovozerskaya pravda,* 25 January, p. 4.

Podol'skaya, A. (1992) 'Ne pora li vernut' dolgi?', *Polyarnaya pravda,* 28 January, p. 2.

Polyarnaya pravda (1995) 'Istok vsemu – sem'ya: Vstretilis' saamy Kol'skogo poluostrova', *Polyarnaya pravda,* 5 April, p. 5.

Povoroznyuk, O., J.O. Habeck and V. Vaté (2010) 'Introduction: On the Definition, Theory, and Practice of Gender Shift in the North of Russia', *The Anthropology of East Europe Review,* 28(2):1–37.

Pridham, G. (1987) 'Interviewing Party-Political Elites in Italy', in G. Moyser and M. Wagstaffe (eds) *Research Methods for Elite Studies,* London: Allen & Unwin, pp. 72–88.

Rahe, J. (1997) 'Sámi: Ein altes Volk hofft auf eine Zukunft', *Westfalen-Blatt,* 28–29 June, p. 1.

Rainwater, L. and D. Pittman (1967) 'Ethical Problems in Studying a Politically Sensitive and Deviant Community', *Social Problems,* 14:357–366.

RAIPON (2006) 'Drugie obshchestvennye organizatsii KMNSS i SV RF'. Retrieved19 August 2011 from http//raipon.org/*АКМНССиДВРФ*/Другиеобщественныеорга низацииКМНС/tabid/297/Default.aspx.

Rantala, L. (1992) 'The Linguistic Situation of the Kola Sámi', in O. Snellman and A. Vuolio (eds) *Third Circumpolar Universities Cooperation Conference 30.11.1992–03.12.1992: Abstracts,* Rovaniemi: University of Lapland, pp. 16–17.

Rantala, L. (1994a) 'De ryska samernas nationella uppvaknande', in Tromsø Museum, *Festskrift til Ørnulf Vorren,* Tromsø: Tromsø Museum, pp. 313–319.

Rantala, L. (1994b) 'Samerna på Kolahalvön – Deras situation i dag', *Journal de la Société Finno-Ougrienne,* 85:200–204.

Rantala, L. (2004) 'Historik'. *Samernas 18. Konferens* [Sami Conference] *Honningsvåg, 7 September 2004,* Samerådet 50 år.

Report to Parliament No. 55 2000–2001: 'St. meld nr 55: Om samepolitikken'. White Paper approved by the Norwegian government on 31 August 2001. Retrieved 16 April 2010 from http//www.regjeringen.no/nb/dep/aid/dok/regpubl/stmeld/20002001/stmeld-nr-55-2000-2001-/7.html?id=325876.

Rießler, M. and J. Wilbur (2007) 'Documenting the Endangered Kola Saami Languages' in T. Bull, J. Kusmenko and M. Rießler (eds) *Språk og språkforhold i Sápmi,* Berlin: Nordeuropa-Institut der Humboldt-Universität.

Robinson, M.P. and K.A.S. Kassam (1998) *Sámi Potatoes: Living with Reindeer and Perestroika,* Calgary: Bayeux Arts.

Rogozina, L. (1989) 'Saami i Komi – vne ocheredy', *Polyarnaya pravda,* 18 October, p. 4.

Rossi, I. (1999) 'Aid for the Kola Sámi', in W. Dallmann (ed.) *NNSIPRA Bulletin,* No. 3, November, p. 32.

Rosstat (2002) *All-Russian Census,* Moscow: Rosstat.

Rybkin, A. (1998) *Indigenous Peoples of Russia: Modern Structure of Self-Organisation and Interactions with State Bodies,* Moscow: World Association of Reindeer Herders and Indigenous Peoples Committee of Barents Region.

Rykova, V. (1990) 'Skazania o noydakh (shamanakh saamov)', *Lovozerskaya pravda,* 18 December, p. 3.

Ryzhova, N. (1997) 'Sokhranit' krasotu i legendy Seidozera', *Murmanskiy vestnik,* 23 August, p. 5.

Sámi instituhtta (1990) 'The Sámi People', Karasjok.

Sámi Parliamentary Conference (2005) 'Declaration from the First Sami Parliamentarian Conference. Jokkmokk, 24 February 2005'. Retrieved 2 April 2010 from http//www.sametinget.se/1433.

Sámi Parliamentary Council (2006) 'SPR Virksomhetsplan 2006–2007. Godtatt på SPR plenum 16.–17.3.2006'. Retrieved 2 April 2010 from http//www.samediggi.no/kunde/filer/SPR%20virksomhetsplan%202006-2007.pdf.

Sarv, M. (1996) 'Changes in the Social Life of the Kola Sámi', in I. Seurujärvi-Kari and U.M. Kulonen (eds) *Essays on Indigenous Identity and Rights,* Helsinki: Helsinki University Press, pp. 131–139.

Sashenkova, L. (1997) 'PU-26 – v Lovozere', *Lovozerskaya pravda,* 6 September, p. 6.

Sashenkova, L. (1998a) 'Rabotat' na doverii: S konferentsii saamov v Lovozere', *Lovozerskaya pravda,* 7 April, p. 5.

Sashenkova, L. (1998b) 'Uchilishche est' i budet', *Lovozerskaya pravda,* 1 May, p. 2.

Sashenkova, L. (1998c) 'Problemy u nas obshchie – kruglyi stol finskikh i rossiskikh masterov i pedagogov profobucheniya molodezhi', *Lovozerskaya pravda,* 10 June, p. 5.

Sashenkova, L. (1998d) 'Zdrastvuy, 'Murman Elme Sam'', *Lovozerskaya pravda,* 17 July, p. 5.

Sashenkova, L. (1998e) 'Sessiya byla ser'yeznoy', *Lovozerskaya pravda,* 30 October, p. 5.

Sashenkova, L. (1998f) 'God prozhit s udachey', *Lovozerskaya pravda,* 27 December, p. 2.

Scheller, E. (2004) *Kolasamiska – språkbyte eller språkbevarande? En sociolingvistisk studie av samernas språksituation i Ryssland,* Umeå: Umeå universitet Sámi dutkan/ Samiska studier.

Scheller, E. (2011) 'The Saami Language Situation in Russia', in *Uralica Helsingensia,* 5:76–96.

Schindler, D. (1992) 'Russian Hegemony and Indigenous Rights in Chukotka', *Inuit Studies,* 16(1–2):51–74.

Schindler, D. (1993) 'Hunters, Herders and Development in the Russian North', in Institute of Ethnography and Anthropology, *Hunters and Gatherers in Modern Context,* Vol. 2, Moscow: Russian Academy of Sciences, pp. 597–606 [from conference held 18–22 August 1993].

Schindler, D. (1997) 'Redefining Tradition and Renegotiating Ethnicity in Native Russia', *Arctic Anthropology,* 34(1):194–211.

Selivanov, V. (1984) 'U saamov skandinavii', *Lovozerskaya pravda,* 7 April, p. 1.

Selivanov, V. (1990) 'Budni Assotsiatsii', *Lovozerskaya pravda,* 1 February, p. 3.

Semisorov, V. (1993) 'Chestnyy biznes i chestnaya informatsiya', *Polyarnaya pravda,* 25 May, p. 2.

Shils, E. (1959/1973) 'Social Inquiry and the Autonomy of the Individual', in D. Lerner (ed.) *The Meaning of the Social Sciences,* Gloucester, MA: Peter Smith, pp. 114–157.

Shumkin, V. (1986) 'Drevneyshaya narodnost'', *Lovozerskaya pravda,* 9 January, p. 2.

Sidorin, V. (1991) 'Kholod – ne kholod, pastukh, kak olen'…', *Polyarnaya pravda,* 6 December, p. 2.

Simonsen, S.G. (1999) 'Inheriting the Soviet Policy Tool Box: Russia's Dilemma Over Ascriptive Nationality', *Europe–Asia Studies,* 51(6):1069–1087.

Skachko, A. (1931) 'Ocherednye zadachi sovetskoi raboty sredi malykh narodov Severa', *Sovetskiy Sever,* 2:5–29.

Slezkine, Yu. (1994) *Arctic Mirrors: Russia and the Small Peoples of the North,* Ithaca: Cornell University Press.

Smirnov, D. (1997) 'Polevaya konferentsiya i rabochaya vstrechya. Natsional'ny park 'Khibiny' – svoimi glazami', *Zhivaya Arktika,* 3(8):10–11.

Smith, A. (1981) *The Ethnic Revival in the Modern World,* Cambridge: Cambridge University Press.

Smith, A. (1995) *Nations and Nationalism in a Global Era,* Cambridge: Polity Press.

Smith, G. (1996) 'The Soviet State and Nationalities Policy', in G. Smith (ed.) *The Nationalities Question in the Post-Soviet States,* London: Longman, pp. 2–22.

Sokolova, Z.P. and A.N. Yakovlev (1998) *Assessment of Social and Cultural Impact on Indigenous Peoples of Expanded Use of the Northern Sea Route,* INSROP Working Paper, No. 111, Oslo: The Fridtjof Nansen Institute.

Sorokazherd'yev, V. (1998) 'Vot i dozhdalsya Chernyakov: Knigu o nashikh saamakh izdali v Finlandii', *Murmanskiy vestnik,* 15 July, p. 3.

SSB (2009) 'Samer i Norge'. Retrieved 19 August 2011 from http//www.ssb.no/ samer/.

Statkart (2011) 'UNESCOs røde liste over truede samiske språk'. Retrieved 19 August 2011 from http//www.statkart.no/?module=Articles;action=Article. publicShow;ID=15437.

Stordahl, V. (1991) 'Ethnic Integration and Identity Management: Discourses of Sámi Self-Awareness', *North Atlantic Studies,* 3(1):25–30.

Stordahl, V. (1994) 'Identity and Sáminess: Expressing World View and Nation', in a special issue of *Dieđut* (1994) *Majority–Minority Relations: The Case of the Sámi in Scandinavia, Conference Report Guovdageaidnu, Norway, 2–4 July 1993,* (1):57–62.

Sveum, T. (ed.) (1988) Østsamer: språk, kultur, historie – *en litteraturoversikt,* Tromsø: Universitetsbibilioteket.

Svonni, M. (1996) 'Saami Language as a Marker of Ethnic Identity among the Saami', in I. Seurujärvi-Kari and U.M. Kulonen (eds) *Essays on Indigenous Identity and Rights,* Helsinki: Helsinki University Press, pp. 105–125.

Swedish Institute (1991) *The Sámi People in Sweden,* Stockholm: The Swedish Institute.

Swedish Sámi Parliament (2009) 'Statistik sameröstlängden'. Retrieved 19 August 2011 from http//www.sametinget.se/6434.

Szynkiewicz, S. (1990) 'Mythologised Representations in Soviet Thinking on the Nationalities Problem', *Anthropology Today,* 6(2):2–5.

Taksami, Ch. (1990a) 'Ethnic Groups of the Soviet North: A General Historical and Ethnographical Description', in D.R.F. Collis (ed.) *Arctic Languages: An Awakening,* Paris: UNESCO, pp. 23–38.

Taksami, Ch. (1990b) 'Opening Speech at the Congress of Small Indigenous Peoples of the Soviet North', in IWGIA *Indigenous Peoples of the Soviet North,* Document No. 67, Copenhagen: IWGIA, pp. 23–45.

Tanner, V. (1929) *Antropogeografiska studier inom Petsamo-området: I Skoltlapparna,* special issue of *Fennia,* 49(4):518.

Terebikhin, N.M. (1993) *Sakral'naya geografiya russkogo severa: Religiozno-mifologicheskoye prostranstvo severnorusskoy kultury,* Arkhangelsk: Izdatel'stvo Pomorskogo mezhdunarodnogo pedagogisheskogo universiteta imeni M.V. Lomonosova.

Tret'yakov, A. (1998) 'Chuzhaya rybalka na nashikh rekakh', *Lovozerskaya pravda,* 22 May, p. 5.

Tsypanov, Je. (1992) 'Linguistic Situation and Language Policy in the Areas Inhabited by Izhma Group of the Komi People', in O. Snellman and A. Vuolio (eds) *Third Circumpolar Universities Cooperation Conference 30.11.1992–03.12.1992: Abstracts,* Rovaniemi: University of Lapland, pp. 19–21.

Tumka, G.S. (1983) 'Polozheniye o gosudarstvennom kompleksnom zakaznike "Seidozero"', Resheniye No. 363, 31 August, Murmansk: Oblispolkom [*oblast* decree].

Ushakov, I. (1975) *Istoriya rodnogo kraya,* Murmansk: Murmanskoye knizhnoye isdatel'stvo.

Ushakov, I. (1996) 'A za belkoyu – lisitsa', *Polyarnaya pravda,* 16 April, p. 4.

Ushakov, I. and S.N. Dashchinskiy (1988) *Lovozero,* Murmansk: Murmanskoye knizhnoye izdatel'stvo.

Utvik, U. (1985) *Kolasamene: Fra tsarens undersåtter til sovjetiske borgere,* Bergen: Russisk institutt, Universitetet i Bergen [*hovedfag* thesis].

Uvachan, V. (1990) 'Socio-Economic and Cultural Development of the Peoples of the North', in D.R.F. Collis (ed.) *Arctic Languages: An Awakening,* Paris: UNESCO, pp. 39–47.

Vakhtin, N. (1994) 'The Native Peoples of the Russian Far North', in Minority Rights Group (ed.) *Polar Peoples: Self-Determination and Development,* London: Minority Rights Publications, pp. 29–104.

Vakhtin, N. (1997) 'Linguistic Situation in the Russian Far North: Language Loss and Language Transformation', in Graduate School of Letters (ed.) *Languages of the North Pacific Rim*, Vol. 2, Kyoto: University of Kyoto, pp. 163–177.

Vászolyi, E.G. (1971) 'Some Thoughts on the National Minorities of the European North of the USSR', *Polar Record*, 15(99):855–861.

Vatonena, L. (1989) 'Soviet Union: The Problem of the Soviet Saami', in IWGIA Newsletter No. 59, December 1989, pp. 89–91 [reprinted from *Lovozerskaya pravda*, 5 November, 1988, p. 3].

Vatonena, L. (1994) 'Samer i Ryssland i dag', *Samefolket*, 74(1):32.

Vdovina, N.S. (1997) 'Bylo i taksi za 500 tyc.', *Lovozerskaya pravda*, 18 April, pp. 4–5.

Vidich, A.J. and J. Bensman (1958) *Small Town in Mass Society*, Princeton: Princeton University Press.

Vitebsky, P. (1989a) 'Reindeer Herders of Northern Yakutia: A Report from the Field', *Polar Record*, 25(154):213–218.

Vitebsky, P. (1989b) 'Perestroika among the Reindeer Herders', *Geographical Magazine*, 61(6):22–24.

Vitebsky, P. (1990a) 'Centralized Decentralization: the Ethnography of Remote Reindeer Herders under Perestroika', *Cahiers du Monde russe et sovietique*, 31(2–3):345–356.

Vitebsky, P. (1990b) 'Gas Environmentalism and Native Anxieties in the Soviet Arctic: The Case of Yamal Peninsula', *Polar Record*, 26(156):19–26.

Vitebsky, P. (1991) 'The Reindeer Herders of Siberia', in P. Carmichael (ed.) *Nomads*, London: Collins and Brown, pp. 125–146.

Vitebsky, P. (1992) 'Landscape and Self-Determination among the Eveny. The Political Environment of Siberian Reindeer Herders Today', in E. Croll and D. Parkin (eds) *Bush Base: Forest Farm – Culture, Environment and Development*, London: Routledge, pp. 223–246.

Vitebsky, P. (1996) 'The Northern Minorities', in G. Smith (ed.) *The Nationalities Question in the Post-Soviet States*, London: Longman, pp. 94–112.

Volkov, N.N. (1946/1996) *The Russian Sami*, Kautokeino: Nordic Sámi Institute [Kunstkamera *kandidatskaya* from 1946, translated and published as special issue of *Diedut*, (2):1–95].

Voronov, A. (1989) 'Association of Kola Saamis Calls for Action', *Northern News*, (13):1–2.

World Reindeer Peoples' Union (1997) 'Forprosjekt *for utarbeidelse av handlingsprogram for reindriften i Murmansk oblast og Nenets A.O.*', Kirkenes: Barentssekretariatet.

Yefremov, I. (1993a) 'Chestnyy biznes – eto chestnoye partnerstvo', *Polyarnaya pravda*, 12 May, p. 1.

Yefremov, I. (1993b) 'Saamskiy zhenskiy uik-end', *Polyarnaya pravda*, 24 July, p. 2.

Yefremov, I. (1995a) 'Inostrannyy rybolovnyy turizm: semuzh'ya voyna', *Polyarnaya pravda*, 15 August, p. 2.

Yefremov, I. (1995b) 'Olenevodstvo mozhet byt' vygodnym', *Polyarnaya pravda*, 19 December, p. 2.

Yefremov, I. (1997a) 'Novyy god v tundre', *Polyarnaya pravda*, 31 December, pp. 1, 2.

Yefremov, I. (1997b) 'Proyekt "Khibiny"', *Polyarnaya pravda*, 26 August, p. 3.

Yefremov, I. (1998a) 'Saamskiy yazyk: Vozrozhdeniye ili reanimatsiya?', *Lovozerskaya pravda*, 24 April, p. 2.

Yefremov, I. (1998b) 'Nel'zya ob"yat' Neob"yatnuyu'?', *Lovozerskaya pravda*, 17 July, p. 5.

Yefremov, I. (1998c) 'V. Sirota: 'Tundra' vozroditsya – ya ne somnevayus', *Lovozerskaya pravda*, 28 August, pp. 1, 2.

Yegorov, Yu. (1992) 'Perevod v selo – pastukhu nakazaniye', *Polyarnaya pravda*, 19 May, p. 3

Yurchak, A. (2006) *Everything Was Forever, Until It Was No More: The Last Soviet Generation*, Princeton: Princeton University Press.

Yushkov, Ya. (1992) 'Oleney – olenevodam', *Lovozerskaya pravda*, 18 February, p. 2.

Zaharov, V. (1994) 'Brev från tundran: Om man vore gift och får en sådan lön – då kan man gå och hänga sig', *Samefolket*, 75(5):34–35.

Zavalko, S. (2011) 'Kola Sámi Demographic Analyses by Sergey Zavalko', in T. Mustonen and K. Mustonen, *Eastern Sámi Atlas*, Vaasa: Oy Fram Ab, pp. 199–203.

Zazulin, A.P. (1982) 'Ob organizatsii kompleksnogo gosudarstvennogo sakaznika "Seidozero"', Resheniye No. 538, 24 November, oblispolkom [*oblast* decree].

Zelensky, M., V. Melnikov, V. Bichkov and I. Zagrebin (1997) *Role of Naukan Native Company in Encouraging Traditional Native Use of Wildlife Resources by Chukotka Natives and in Conducting Shore Based Observations on the Distribution of Bowhead Whales, Balaena mysticetus, in Coastal Waters off the South-Eastern Part of the Chukotka Peninsula*, Barrow: Department of Wildlife Management.

Zherebtsov, I.L. (1992) 'Life Conditions and Social Policy in the Areas Inhabited by the Komi-Izhma People', in O. Snellman and A. Vulio (eds) *Third Circumpolar Universities Cooperation Conference 30.11.1992–03.12.1992: Abstracts*, Rovaniemi: University of Lapland, pp. 20–21.

Zherebtsov, L. N. (1982) *Istoriko-kul'urnyye vzaimnootnosheniya Komi c sosednimi narodami*, Moscow: Nauka.

Zorgdrager, N. (1984) 'The Saami People', in G.W. Nooter (ed.) *Life and Survival in the Arctic*, The Hague: Government Publishing Office, pp. 11–44.

INDEX